PARTITION-BASED TRAPDOOR CIPHERS

Authored by **Arnaud Bannier** and **Eric Filiol**

Partition-based Trapdoor Ciphers
http://dx.doi.org/10.5772/intechopen.69485
Authored by Arnaud Bannier and Eric Filiol

Scientific Reviewer

Jaydip Sen

Published by InTech

Janeza Trdine 9, 51000 Rijeka, Croatia

Publishing Process Manager Viktorija Zgela
Technical Editor SPi Global
Cover InTech Design team

First published September, 2017
Printed in Croatia
Legal deposit, Croatia: National and University Library in Zagreb

Additional hard copies can be obtained from orders@intechopen.com

Partition-based Trapdoor Ciphers, Authored by Arnaud Bannier and Eric Filiol
p. cm.
Print ISBN 978-953-51-3386-5
Online ISBN 978-953-51-3385-8

For EU product safety concerns:
IN TECH d.o.o., Prolaz Marije Krucifikse Kozulić 3, 51000 Rijeka, Croatia,
info@intechopen.com or visit our website at intechopen.com.

Meet the authors

Professor Eric Filiol is the head of the Operational Cryptology and Virology research lab (C+V)° at ESIEA, France and a senior consultant in offensive cybersecurity and intelligence. He spent 22 years in the French Army (Infantry/Marine Corps). He holds an engineer diploma in cryptology, a PhD in applied mathematics and computer science, and a habilitation thesis in computer science. He graduated from NATO in InfoOps and Intelligence. He is the Editor-in-Chief of the Journal of Computer Virology and Hacking Techniques. Prof. Filiol has been a speaker at various international security events including Black Hat, CCC, CanSecWest, PacSec, Hack.lu, Brucon, H2HC... His research areas include cryptography, computer virology, intelligence and cyberwarfare techniques.

Arnaud Bannier is a lecturer and researcher at (C+V)° research lab at ESIEA, France. He holds a master's degree in cryptology from the Rennes 1 University. He is now concluding its PhD thesis in computer science which deals with block ciphers.

Contents

Partition-Based Trapdoor Ciphers

Arnaud Bannier and Eric Filiol

Additional information is available at the end of the chapter

http://dx.doi.org/10.5772/intechopen.70420

Abstract

Trapdoors are a two-face key concept in modern cryptography. They are primarily related to the concept of trapdoor function used in asymmetric cryptography. A trapdoor function is a one-to-one mapping that is easy to compute, but for which its inverse function is difficult to compute without special information, called the trapdoor. It is a necessary condition to get reversibility between the sender and the receiver for encryption or between the signer and the verifier for digital signature. The trapdoor mechanism is always fully public and detailed. The second concept of trapdoor relates to the more subtle and perverse concept of mathematical backdoor, which is a key issue in symmetric cryptography. In this case, the aim is to insert hidden mathematical weaknesses, which enable one who knows them to break the cipher. Therefore, the existence of a backdoor is a strongly undesirable property. This book deals with this second concept and is focused on block ciphers or, more specifically, on substitution-permutation networks (SPN). Inserting a backdoor in an encryption algorithm gives an effective cryptanalysis of the cipher to the designer.

Keywords: cryptography, block ciphers, backdoor, trapdoor, substitution-permutation network, cryptanalysis

Preface

1. Introduction

Despite the fact that in the late 90s/early 2000s, citizens have partially obtained the freedom for using cryptography, the recent years have shown that more than ever, governments and intelligence agencies still try to control and bypass the cryptographic means used for the protection of data and of private life. Snowden leaks have been a first upheaval. A tremendous number of secret projects conducted by NSA and GCHQ have been revealed to the public opinion. They have shed a new light on the permanent attempt to control the use of cryptography by a growing number of governments.

The recurring approaches and attempts consist in making the implementation of backdoors mandatory. The simplest and naive approach consists in enforcing key escrowing at the operators' level. But point-to-point encryption solutions like telegram, signal or proton mail enable to prevent it. A number of different backdoor techniques are regularly mentioned or proposed.

The most critical aspect in embedding backdoors lies on the fact that hackers or analysts may find them more or less easily and worse may exploit them. This is the reason why operators or developers are very reluctant to accept backdoors until now. In case of leak, they inevitably lose users' confidence and favor the development of trusted services abroad. In fact, the backdoor issue arises due to the fact that only implementation backdoors (at the protocol/implementation/management level) are generally considered.

In this book, we address the most critical issue of backdoors: mathematical or by-design backdoors. In other words, the backdoor is put directly in the mathematical design of the encryption algorithm. While the algorithm is totally public, proving that there is a backdoor, identifying it and exploiting it, is generally an intractable problem, unless you know the backdoor [1]. To some extent, the RSA's `Dual_EC_DRBG` standard case falls within this category [2]. Other nonpublic examples are known within the military cryptanalysis community and partially revealed to the public, thanks to the 1995 Hans Buehler case [3]. This kind of backdoor is the most difficult one to address and there is quite no public work on that topic. It is generally the technical realm of a few among the most eminent intelligence agencies, namely NSA and GCHQ, which moreover have the ability and power to step in and to influence the international standardization processes. Our objective is to explain that it is probably possible to design and put such backdoors. In this book, we consider a particular case among many other possibilities of trapdoors.

This book is organized as follows. In the next section, we explore the concept of backdoors and trapdoors and we identify two main categories. We also present the state-of-the-art, history and previous work regarding backdoors, mostly in symmetric cryptography. The rest of this book focuses on substitution-permutation networks (or SPN for short) which are a special class of block encryption systems, mapping a partition of the plaintexts to a partition of the ciphertexts, independently of the round keys used.

Chapter 2 explores the concept of linear partitions and their relationships with substitution-permutation networks. We show in Section 2 that in our case, the study of the full cipher can be restricted to the substitution layer without loss of generality. Then in Section 3, we explore this latter primitive and show that the problem can be restricted further to the study of a single S-box.

In Chapter 3, we discuss how to design a suitable S-box which preserves a linear partition and, at the same time, which resists linear and differential cryptanalysis. From those theoretical results, we have designed a full AES-like encryption system, called BEA-1, presented in Chapter 4. Section 1 gives the full specifications of this cipher. Then Section 2 deals with the design of its backdoor. In Section 3, we sketch the basic ideas underlying the BEA-1 cryptanalysis while in Section 4, we present our cryptanalysis of BEA-1 under the assumption we have the full knowledge of the backdoor.

Chapter 5 concludes this book and explore new ideas and trends in encryption backdoors. The full description of cryptographic primitives used in BEA-1 is given in Appendix.

2. The concept of backdoor

2.1. Definition and classification proposal

Trapdoors are a two-face key concept in modern cryptography. They are primarily related to the concept of *trapdoor function* used in asymmetric cryptography. A trapdoor function is a one-to-one mapping that is easy to compute, but for which its inverse function is difficult to compute without special information, called the *trapdoor*. It is a necessary condition to get reversibility between the sender and the receiver for encryption or between the signer and the verifier for digital signature. The trapdoor mechanism is always fully public and detailed. The security and the core principle are based on the existence of a secret information, the private key, which is essentially part of the trapdoor. In other words, the private key can be seen as *the* trapdoor.

The second concept of trapdoor relates to the more subtle and perverse concept of *mathematical backdoor*, which is a key issue in symmetric cryptography. In this case, the aim is to insert hidden mathematical weaknesses which enable one who knows them to break the cipher. Nonetheless, mathematical backdoors may be extended to asymmetric cryptography, see for example the case of the `DUAL EC_DRBG` [2], or the case of trapdoor primes addresses recently in [4]. Therefore, the existence of a backdoor is a strongly undesirable property.

In the rest of this section, we will oppose the term of trapdoor, the desirable property, to that of backdoor, the undesirable one. While the term of trapdoor has been already used in the very few literature covering the second face of this problem, we suggest however to use the term of backdoor to describe the issue of hidden mathematical weaknesses. This would avoid ambiguity and maybe would favor the research work around a topic which is nowadays mostly addressed by governmental entities in the context of cryptography control and regulations.

Inserting backdoors in encryption algorithms underlies quite systematically the choice of cryptographic standards (DES, AES...). The reason is that the testing, validation and selection processes are always conducted by governmental entities (NIST or equivalent) with the technical support of secret entities (NSA or equivalent). So an interesting and critical research area is: "how easy and feasible is it to design and to insert backdoors in encryption algorithms?". In this book, we intend to address one very particular case of this question. It is important to keep in mind that a backdoor may be itself defined in the following two ways.

- As a "natural weakness" known, but none disclosed, only by the tester, validator or final decision-maker. The best historic example is that of the differential cryptanalysis. Following Biham and Shamir's seminal work in 1991 [5], NSA acknowledged that it was aware of that cryptanalysis years ago [6]. Most of experts estimate that it was nearly 20 years ahead. However a number of non public, commercial block ciphers in the early 90s might have been be weak with respect to differential cryptanalysis.
- As an intended design weakness put by the author of the algorithm. To the authors knowledge, there is no known case for public algorithms yet.

As far as symmetric cryptography is concerned, there are two major families of cipher systems for which the issue of backdoor must be considered differently.

- *Stream ciphers*. Their design complexity is rather low since they mostly rely on algebraic primitives: LFSRs and Boolean functions which have intensely been studied in the open literature Until the late 70s, backdoors relied on the fact that quite all algorithms were proprietary and hence secret. It was then easy to hide nonprimitive polynomials, weak-combining Boolean functions... The Hans Buehler case in 1995 [3] shed light on that particular case.
- *Block ciphers*. This class of encryption algorithms is rather recent (end of the 70s for the public part). They exhibit so a huge combinatorial complexity that it is reasonable to think to backdoors. As described in [7] for a κ-bit secret key and an m-bit input/output block cipher there are $((2^m)!)^{2^\kappa}$ possible such block ciphers. For such an algorithm, the number of possible internal states is so huge that we are condemned to have only a local view of the system, that is, the round function or the basic cryptographic primitives. We cannot be sure that there is no degeneration effect at a higher level. This point has been addressed in [7] when considering linear cryptanalysis. Therefore, it seems reasonable to think that this combinatorial richness of block ciphers may be used to hide backdoors.

Since block ciphers are now the most widely used encryption algorithms by the general public and the industry, we will focus on them in the rest of this book. Backdoors in stream ciphers have quite never been exposed to the public.

2.2. Previous work

Regarding the previous work, we can consider two aspects. The first one relates to authors who have considered structures on the input and output spaces of round functions to build key distinguishing or key recovery attacks. In this case, it is possible to suppose that those structures are "natural" structures. The second case is directly linked to the topic covered in this book. It relates to the design of backdoors based on such structures. Exploiting these hidden structures then leads to a tractable cryptanalysis. In this respect, we can see those structures as "intended" and no longer "natural".

2.2.1. *Attacks using space structures*

Among the very first previous works that have considered structures in the plaintext and ciphertext spaces is the contribution of Evertse [8]. This paper introduced the linear structures for block ciphers, which map a subspace of $\mathbb{F}_2^m \times \mathbb{F}_2^\kappa$ (the product of the plaintext and ciphertext spaces) onto a subspace of $\mathbb{F}_2^m$ (the ciphertext space). Then, the author showed that if such a linear structure exists, then known-plaintext and chosen-plaintext attacks faster than exhaustive search are possible.

Later, Leander et al. [9] developed a new cryptanalysis, called *invariant subspace attack*, breaking the PRINTCIPHER [10] for a significant fraction of its keys. The general idea of this attack can be outlined as follows. Let F denote the SP-layer of a substitution-permutation network, that is, the round function without the key addition. Then, assume that F maps a coset of a given subspace V to another coset of V. In other words, there exist a and b such that $F(a+V) = b+V$. Here, the addition is made in $\mathbb{F}_2^n$ and hence corresponds with the XOR operation. The round function associated with the round key k is then defined by $F_k : x \mapsto F(x+k)$. If the round key k belongs to the coset $a + b + V$, then it holds that

$$F_k(b+V) = F(b+k+V) = F(a+V) = b+V,$$

hence the name of *invariant subspace*. Therefore, if every round key lies in this particular coset, the affine subspace $b + V$ is preserved by the full encryption process. Such a property enables a very efficient distinguisher. As additional results, they also showed that the invariant subspace attack

- implies a truncated differential attack to be possible (the probability of the truncated differential characteristic is however highly key-dependent);
- implies the existence of strongly biased linear approximations for weak keys (independently of the number of rounds).

This attack has been generalized in 2015 by Leander et al. [11]. They proposed a generic algorithm that is able to detect invariant subspaces. Indeed, their initial invariant subspaces on PRINTCIPHER were found empirically.

Following the idea of the invariant subspace attack, Grassi et al. [12] introduced the *subspace trail cryptanalysis*. Given $r + 1$ subspaces $V^{[0]}, \ldots, V^{[r]}$, it is assumed that the image of any coset of $V^{[i]}$ under the SP-network is included in a coset of $V^{[i+1]}$. That is to say, for each $a^{[i]}$, there exists $a^{[i+1]}$ such the following inclusion holds

$$F(a^{[i]} + V^{[i]}) \subseteq a^{[i+1]} + V^{[i+1]}.$$

In this case, it is easy to see the all round functions F_k inherit such a property. The family of subspaces $(V^{[i]})_{i \le r}$ is said to be a *subspace trail*. Naturally, the dimension of $V^{[i]}$ must be lower

Work	Structure	Key dependence
Evertse [8]	Linear structure (if any)	Key independent
Leander et al. [9, 11]	Exact coset	Round key dependent
Grassi et al. [12]	Coset independent	Round key independent
Our approach	Coset independent	Round key independent

Table 1.1. Comparison of existing work with respect to input and output space structures.

than or equal to the dimension of $V^{[i+1]}$. In contrast to the invariant subspace attack, Grassi et al. relaxed the assumption that the coset has to be invariant. Here, the considered subset becomes the coset of possibly different increasingly dimensional subspaces throughout the encryption. However, the authors also required this property to hold for each coset of $V^{[0]}$ instead of one. Therefore, this cryptanalysis is not a generalization but a variation of the invariant subspace attack. As will become clear in Section 2 of Chapter 2, the family of backdoors covered in this book is closely related to constant-dimensional subspace trails.

Let us mention that in [13], the authors introduced nonlinear invariant subspaces by considering a general Boolean function g such that $g(F(x)) \oplus g(x)$ is constant. Finally, **Table 1.1** summarized the structures considered by the attacks presented in this section and compared it with our work.

2.2.2. Backdoor design and structures

One of the first trapdoor ciphers was created in 1997 by Rijmen and Preneel [14]. Their S-boxes are constructed to have one high correlation between the zero mapping and a sum of certain output bits. The knowledge of this correlation yields a high potential linear trail which is used to recover a part of the key with linear cryptanalysis. Such a weakness is generally pointed out by the first line of the S-boxes' correlation matrices. Yet, if the output size of the S-boxes is large enough, their computation is too expensive. Relying on this fact, the authors claimed that their trapdoor is undetectable, even if one knows its global design. Nevertheless, Wu et al. [15] disproved this by discovering a way to recover the trapdoor. It is worthwhile to mention that in practice, if a real cipher containing a trapdoor is given, the presence of the trapdoor will certainly not be revealed.

More recently in [16], the authors created non-surjective S-boxes embedding a parity check to create a trapdoor cipher. The message space is thus divided into cosets and leads to create an attack on this DES-like cipher in less than 2^{23} operations. The security of the whole algorithm, particularly against linear and differential cryptanalysis is not given and the authors admit that their attack is dependent on the first and last permutation of the cipher. Finally, the non-surjective S-boxes may lead to detect easily the trapdoor by simply calculating the image of each input vector. This problem is naturally avoided in a substitution-permutation network in which S-boxes are bijective by definition.

Our approach is mainly a generalization of the ideas presented by Paterson in [17]. In this article, a DES-like trapdoor cipher exploiting a weakness induced by the round functions is presented. The group generated by the round functions acts imprimitively on the message space. In other words, the round function preserves a partition of the message space no matter the round key used, and hence, the same applies to the full cipher. This partition forms the trapdoor. Paterson then introduced a trapdoor cipher composed of 32 rounds and using an 80-bit key. The trapdoor enables recovery of the key using 2^{41} operations and 2^{32} chosen plaintexts. Even if the mathematical material to build the trapdoor is given, no general algorithm details the S-boxes' construction. Furthermore, as the author says, S-boxes using these principles are incomplete: half of the ciphertext bits are independent of half of the plaintext bits. Finally, the security against a differential attack is said to be *not as high as one might expect*. Moreover, the author wondered whether the partition of the message space had to be linear, that is to say, made up with every coset of a linear subspace. Caranti et al. [18] provided a first answer to Paterson's question, by proving that if the group generated by the round functions is imprimitive, then the partition of the message space must be linear. In his thesis [19], Harpes considered trapdoor ciphers mapping a partition of the plaintexts to a partition of the ciphertexts. As these partitions are not necessarily equal, this family generalizes Paterson's one. Harpes suggested using this trapdoor with its partitioning cryptanalysis.

Partition-Based Trapdoor Cipher

This chapter intends to study Substitution-Permutation Networks mapping a partition of the plaintexts to a partition of the ciphertexts, independently of the round keys used. All the results of this and the following chapters comes from [20].

1. Linear partitions

Let us begin with some notations and conventions.

Notation 2.1. Let m and n denote positive integers. For two maps f and g, the composition $g \circ f$ (or simply gf) denotes the evaluation of f followed by g. For any set E, let $\#E$ denotes its cardinality. If F is a subset of E, F^c denotes its complement.

Let us denote the Galois field of order two by $\mathbb{F}_2$ and $0_n = (0,\ldots,0)$ the zero vector of $\mathbb{F}_2^n$. All the vector spaces considered in this chapter are over the finite field $\mathbb{F}_2$. It is worthwhile to mention that $(\mathbb{F}_2^n)^m$ will be often identified with $\mathbb{F}_2^{nm}$. The concatenation of two vectors x and y is denoted by $(x \mid\mid y)$.

An n-bit S-box is any permutation of $\mathbb{F}_2^n$. If x and y are two elements of $\mathbb{F}_2^n$, then $\langle x, y\rangle = \sum_{i=0}^{n-1} x_i y_i$. If $L : \mathbb{F}_2^n \to \mathbb{F}_2^m$ is a linear map, define $L^\intercal : \mathbb{F}_2^m \to \mathbb{F}_2^n$ by $\langle L^\intercal(x), y\rangle = \langle x, L(y)\rangle$ for every $(x, y) \in \mathbb{F}_2^n \times \mathbb{F}_2^m$. In other words, $L^\intercal$ is the transpose of L for the bilinear form $\langle \cdot , \cdot \rangle$.

Finally, we will denote the elements of $\mathbb{F}_2^n$ using the hexadecimal notation. For instance, the element $(1, 0, 1, 1, 1)$ of $\mathbb{F}_2^5$ is denoted by 17.

Since we are concerned with ciphers that associate a partition of the ciphertext space to another partition of the plaintext space, let us introduce the following definition.

Definition 2.2. Let f be a permutation of E and $\mathcal{A}$, $\mathcal{B}$ be two partitions of E. Let $f(\mathcal{A})$ denote the set $\{f(A) | A \in \mathcal{A}\}$. We say that f maps $\mathcal{A}$ to $\mathcal{B}$ if $f(\mathcal{A}) = \mathcal{B}$. If $\mathcal{A} = \mathcal{B}$, we says that f *preserves* the partition $\mathcal{A}$.

The two partitions $\{\{x\} \mid x \in E\}$ and $\{E\}$ are called the *trivial partitions* of E. Observe that, for any permutation f of E,

$$f(\{\{x\} \mid x \in E\}) = \{\{x\} \mid x \in E\} \quad \text{and} \quad f(\{E\}) = \{E\}\,.$$

That is, every permutation preserves the two trivial partitions. Moreover it should be highlighted that if f maps $\mathcal{A}$ to $\mathcal{B}$ and if $\mathcal{A}$ is nontrivial, then so is $\mathcal{B}$.

Example 2.3. Let E denote the set $[\![0, 8[\![$ and consider the two partitions $\mathcal{A}$, $\mathcal{B}$ of E defined by $\mathcal{A} = \{\{0, 1, 4\}, \{2, 6\}, \{3, 7\}, \{5\}\}$ and $\mathcal{B} = \{\{0, 2, 7\}, \{1\}, \{3, 5\}, \{4, 6\}\}$. Let f be the permutation of E defined by

$$0 \mapsto 7, \quad 1 \mapsto 0, \quad 2 \mapsto 3, \quad 3 \mapsto 6, \quad 4 \mapsto 2, \quad 5 \mapsto 1, \quad 6 \mapsto 5, \quad 7 \mapsto 4.$$

By definition,

$$\begin{aligned} f(\mathcal{A}) = \{f(A)|A \in \mathcal{A}\} &= \{f(\{0,1,4\}), f(\{2,6\}), f(\{3,7\}), f(\{5\})\} \\ &= \{ \quad \{7,0,2\}, \quad \{3,5\}, \quad \{6,4\}, \quad \{1\}\}. \end{aligned}$$

The equality $f(\mathcal{A}) = \mathcal{B}$ holds, and thus f maps the partition $\mathcal{A}$ to $\mathcal{B}$. ▲

Lemma 2.4. Let f be a permutation of E and $\mathcal{A}$, $\mathcal{B}$ be two partitions of E. If for any part A of $\mathcal{A}$, $f(A)$ is a part of $\mathcal{B}$, then f maps $\mathcal{A}$ to $\mathcal{B}$.

In this chapter, we will consider a special kind of partitions that is composed of all the cosets of a linear subspace. Such partitions have already been introduced by [19, Definition 4.4] and are recalled below.

Definition 2.5 (linear partition). Let $\mathcal{A}$ be a partition of $\mathbb{F}_2^n$. Let V denote its part containing 0_n. The partition $\mathcal{A}$ is said to be *linear* if V is a subspace of $\mathbb{F}_2^n$ and if every part of $\mathcal{A}$ is a coset of V in $\mathbb{F}_2^n$, in other words, if

$$\mathcal{A} = \{x + V | x \in \mathbb{F}_2^n\} = \mathbb{F}_2^n / V.$$

We denote $\mathcal{L}(V)$ such a partition.

Remark 2.6. It turns out that the linear partitions associated with the two trivial subspaces of $\mathbb{F}_2^n$, that is $\{0_n\}$ and $\mathbb{F}_2^n$, correspond with the two trivial partitions of $\mathbb{F}_2^n$. Moreover, if V is a nontrivial subspace of $\mathbb{F}_2^n$, then the linear partition $\mathcal{L}(V)$ is also nontrivial.

Example 2.7. Consider the subspaces V and W of $\mathbb{F}_2^5$ defined by

$$V = \text{span}(\texttt{07}, \texttt{1A}) = \{\texttt{00}, \texttt{07}, \texttt{1A}, \texttt{1D}\} \quad \text{and} \quad W = \text{span}(\texttt{0E}, \texttt{12}) = \{\texttt{00}, \texttt{0E}, \texttt{12}, \texttt{1C}\}.$$

Since both V and W are two-dimensional subspaces of $\mathbb{F}_2^5$, the quotient spaces $\mathcal{L}(V) = \mathbb{F}_2^5/V$ and $\mathcal{L}(W) = \mathbb{F}_2^5/W$ are three-dimensional. In other words, the two linear partitions $\mathcal{L}(V)$ and $\mathcal{L}(W)$ have $2^3 = 8$ parts. It can be verified that

$$\begin{aligned} \mathcal{L}(V) &= \{V, \texttt{01}+V, \texttt{02}+V, \texttt{03}+V, \texttt{08}+V, \texttt{09}+V, \texttt{0A}+V, \texttt{0B}+V\}, \\ \mathcal{L}(W) &= \{W, \texttt{01}+W, \texttt{02}+W, \texttt{03}+W, \texttt{04}+W, \texttt{05}+W, \texttt{06}+W, \texttt{07}+W\}. \end{aligned}$$

For instance, the part $\texttt{0B} + V$ of the linear partition $\mathcal{L}(V)$ is the coset of V with respect to $\texttt{0B}$. Explicitly, it is equal to

$$\texttt{0B} + V = \{\texttt{0B}+\texttt{00}, \texttt{0B}+\texttt{07}, \texttt{0B}+\texttt{1A}, \texttt{0B}+\texttt{1D}\} = \{\texttt{0B}, \texttt{0C}, \texttt{11}, \texttt{16}\}.$$

Now, consider the permutation f of $\mathbb{F}_2^5$ given in **Figure 2.1.** The image of $\texttt{0B} + V$ under f is

$$\begin{aligned} f(\texttt{0B}+V) &= f(\{\texttt{0B}, \texttt{0C}, \texttt{11}, \texttt{16}\}) = \{\texttt{0D}, \texttt{03}, \texttt{11}, \texttt{1F}\} \\ &= \{\texttt{03}+\texttt{0E}, \texttt{03}+\texttt{00}, \texttt{03}+\texttt{12}, \texttt{03}+\texttt{1F}\} = \texttt{03}+W. \end{aligned}$$

		.0	.1	.2	.3	.4	.5	.6	.7	.8	.9	.A	.B	.C	.D	.E	.F
$f(x)$	0.	1E	08	04	13	0F	18	14	10	19	15	0E	0D	03	1C	07	17
	1.	12	11	0B	1B	09	05	1F	00	0A	01	02	1A	06	0C	1D	16

Figure 2.1. The permutation f of Example 2.7.

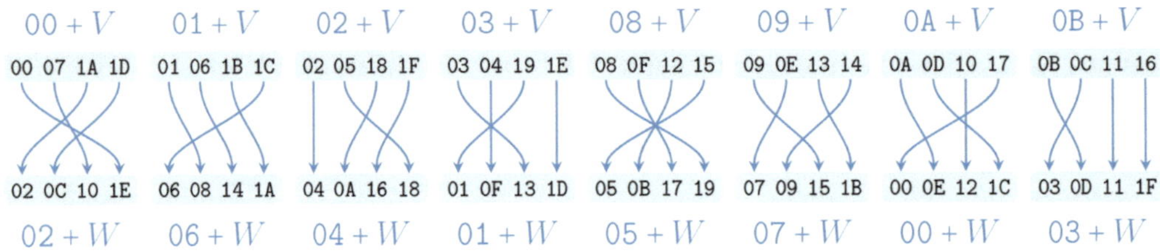

Figure 2.2. The permutation f mapping $\mathcal{L}(V)$ to $\mathcal{L}(W)$ where $V = \text{span}(\texttt{07}, \texttt{1A})$ and $W = \text{span}(\texttt{0E}, \texttt{12})$.

Observe that $f(\texttt{0B} + V)$ is a coset of W so a part of $\mathcal{L}(W)$. The images of all cosets of V under f are displayed in **Figure 2.2.** Since any of them is a part of $\mathcal{L}(W)$, the permutation f maps $\mathcal{L}(V)$ to $\mathcal{L}(W)$. It is worthwhile to observe that a permutation mapping a linear partition to another one does not need to be itself linear or even affine. Indeed, f is certainly not linear as $f(00) = 1E \neq 00$. By contradiction, suppose that f is an affine transformation. Then, there exist a linear mapping $L : \mathbb{F}_2^5 \to \mathbb{F}_2^5$ and an element c of $\mathbb{F}_2^5$ such that $f(x) = L(x) + c$ holds for all x in $\mathbb{F}_2^5$. Therefore,

$$f(x) + f(y) + f(z) = L(x) + c + L(y) + c + L(z) + c = L(x + y + z) + c = f(x + y + z)$$

for all x, y and z in $\mathbb{F}_2^5$. Observe that

$$f(\texttt{00}) + f(\texttt{01}) + f(\texttt{02}) = \texttt{1E} + \texttt{08} + \texttt{04} = \texttt{12} \quad \neq \quad \texttt{13} = f(\texttt{00} + \texttt{01} + \texttt{02}).$$

Thus, f is not an affine transformation. ▲

Lemma 2.8. Let V, W be two subspaces of $\mathbb{F}_2^n$ and f be a permutation of $\mathbb{F}_2^n$, which maps $\mathcal{L}(V)$ to $\mathcal{L}(W)$. For any x in $\mathbb{F}_2^n$, f maps $x + V$ to $f(x) + W$.

Example 2.9. In Example 2.7, we have seen that $f(\texttt{0B} + V) = \texttt{03} + W$. Since f maps $\mathcal{L}(V)$ to $\mathcal{L}(W)$, the previous lemma states that $f(\texttt{0B} + V) = f(\texttt{0B}) + W = \texttt{0D} + W$. There is however no contradiction here because 0D belongs to $\texttt{03} + W$. Consequently, the cosets $\texttt{03} + W$ and $\texttt{0D} + W$ are equal. ▲

The following two propositions are interesting properties of linear partitions, which will be used in the rest of this chapter.

Proposition 2.10. Let V_1, V_2, W_1, W_2 be four subspaces of $\mathbb{F}_2^n$ and f be a permutation of $\mathbb{F}_2^n$, which maps $\mathcal{L}(V_1)$ to $\mathcal{L}(W_1)$ and $\mathcal{L}(V_2)$ to $\mathcal{L}(W_2)$. Then f maps $\mathcal{L}(V_1 \cap V_2)$ to $\mathcal{L}(W_1 \cap W_2)$.

Proposition 2.11. Let V, W be two subspaces of $\mathbb{F}_2^n$ and f be a permutation of $\mathbb{F}_2^n$, which maps $\mathcal{L}(V)$ to $\mathcal{L}(W)$. There exists an automorphism L of $\mathbb{F}_2^n$ such that $L(V) = W$. In particular, V and W are isomorphic.

Example 2.12. Consider again the permutation f of $\mathbb{F}_2^5$ defined in **Figure 2.8.** As seen in the previous example, the permutation maps the linear partition $\mathcal{L}(V)$ to $\mathcal{L}(W)$. Then, Proposition 2.11 ensures that there exists a linear permutation L of $\mathbb{F}_2^5$ such that $L(V) = W$. Consider the bases (`07,1A`) and (`0E,12`) of V and W respectively and complete them into the following bases of $\mathbb{F}_2^5$

$$\mathcal{B}_V = (v_i)_{i<5} = (\texttt{07, 1A, 01, 02, 08}) \quad \text{and} \quad \mathcal{B}_W = (w_i)_{i<5} = (\texttt{0E, 12, 01, 02, 04}).$$

Then, the mapping L can be defined by $L(v_i) = w_i$ for each $i < 5$. This linear transformation will be used in the next chapter. ▲

2. Substitution-permutation networks and partitions

This section aims at studying an SPN, which maps a partition of the plaintexts to a partition of the ciphertexts. When the cipher key K is fixed, the encryption function E_K is just a permutation of the message space. Therefore, any partition $\mathcal{A}$ of the plaintexts is mapped to the partition $E_K(\mathcal{A})$ of the ciphertexts. Nonetheless, to exploit the trapdoor, the designer needs to know the pair of partitions $(\mathcal{A}, E_K(\mathcal{A}))$. The problem is that the output partition $E_K(\mathcal{A})$ depends *a priori* on the cipher key K, which is unknown to the attacker. The simplest way to solve this problem is to require the partition $E_K(\mathcal{A})$ to be independent of the cipher key K. In other words, we want all the partitions $E_K(\mathcal{A})$ to be equal to a fixed partition $\mathcal{B}$.

As with differential and linear cryptanalysis, taking account of the exact effect of the key schedule seems to be a challenging problem. Therefore, the key schedule will deliberately be omitted throughout this chapter. This amounts to consider an SPN mapping a partition $\mathcal{A}$ to a fixed partition $\mathcal{B}$, independently of the round keys used.

2.1. The key addition and diffusion layer

Substitution-permutation networks belong to the class of iterated block ciphers. As every iterated block cipher, the encryption function consists in applying a simple keyed operation called *round function* several times. A different *round key* is used for each iteration of the round function. In practice, these rounds keys are extracted from a master key using an algorithm called *key schedule*. In an SPN, the round function is made up of three distinct stages: a *key addition*, a *substitution layer* and a *permutation* or *diffusion layer*. The substitution layer consists of the parallel evaluation of several S-boxes and is the only part of the cipher, which is not linear or affine. Then, the diffusion layer is the evaluation of some linear mappings (generally one).

Before tackling the full cipher, we look at its basic operations and primitives. The attacker knows the specifications of the substitution and diffusion layers, but he does not know the round key used in the key addition. Therefore, the key addition should not be considered as one operation but rather as a family of permutations. To get back to the subject at hand, we must first determine the partitions $\mathcal{A}$, which are mapped to a unique partition under the action of all round keys.

The next proposition explains the fundamental property of linear partitions according to the key addition. This result was introduced by Harpes in [19]. Later, Caranti et al. gave a similar result expressed for imprimitive groups in [18]. For convenience, we restate this result with our own notations.

Proposition 2.13. Let n be a positive integer. Let $\mathcal{A}$ and $\mathcal{B}$ be two partitions of $\mathbb{F}_2^n$. For each k in $\mathbb{F}_2^n$, let α_k denote the permutation of $\mathbb{F}_2^n$ defined by $\alpha_k(x) = x + k$. Then, the permutation α_k maps $\mathcal{A}$ to $\mathcal{B}$ for any k in $\mathbb{F}_2^n$ if and only if $\mathcal{A} = \mathcal{B}$ and $\mathcal{A}$ is a linear partition.

Even if this result was easily obtained, it has maybe the most important impact on our study. Due to this result and its generalization given later in the next section, only linear partitions will be considered. By definition, the linear partitions are quotient spaces and hence highly structured algebraic objects. Consequently, the apparent combinatorial aspect of our study is reduced to an algebraic problem. This result is indeed quite restrictive since the linear partitions account for a small proportion of all partitions.

Example 2.14. Let n and k be nonnegative integers and q be a prime power. The q-binomial (or Gaussian) coefficient is defined by

$$\begin{bmatrix} n \\ d \end{bmatrix}_q = \prod_{i=1}^{d} \frac{1 - q^{n-i+1}}{1 - q^i}.$$

It can be proved that this coefficient counts the number of d-dimensional subspaces of an n-dimensional vector space over the finite field $\mathbb{F}_q$. Therefore, the number of subspaces of $\mathbb{F}_2^3$ is given by

$$\begin{aligned}\sum_{d=0}^{3} \begin{bmatrix} 3 \\ d \end{bmatrix}_2 &= 1 + \frac{1-2^3}{1-2} + \frac{(1-2^3)(1-2^2)}{(1-2)(1-2^2)} + \frac{(1-2^3)(1-2^2)(1-2^1)}{(1-2)(1-2^2)(1-2^3)} \\ &= 1 + 7 + 7 + 1 = 16.\end{aligned}$$

Since a linear partition of $\mathbb{F}_2^3$ is uniquely determined by a subspace of $\mathbb{F}_2^3$, there are exactly 16 linear partitions. All these partitions are represented graphically at the top of **Figure 2.3.** For instance, the linear partition associated with the subspace $\text{span}(2,4) = \{0,2,4,6\}$ is $\mathcal{L}(\text{span}(2,4)) = \{\{0,2,4,6\},\{1,3,5,7\}\}$.

Proposition 2.13 states that among the set of all the partitions of $\mathbb{F}_2^n$, only the linear ones yield a unique output partition for every key. The Bell number B_m counts the number of partitions of a set of size m. Thus, the number of partitions of $\mathbb{F}_2^n$ is B_{2^n}. For $n = 3$, there are $B_8 = 4140$ partitions in all. Hence, the linear partitions represent a fraction of $16/B_8 \approx 2^{-8.0}$. This ratio falls greatly as n increases. In fact, for $n = 4$, only $67/B_{16} \approx 2^{-27.2}$ are linear and for $n = 5$, this ratio becomes $374/B_{32} \approx 2^{-78.2}$. This underlines how Proposition 2.13 is restrictive.

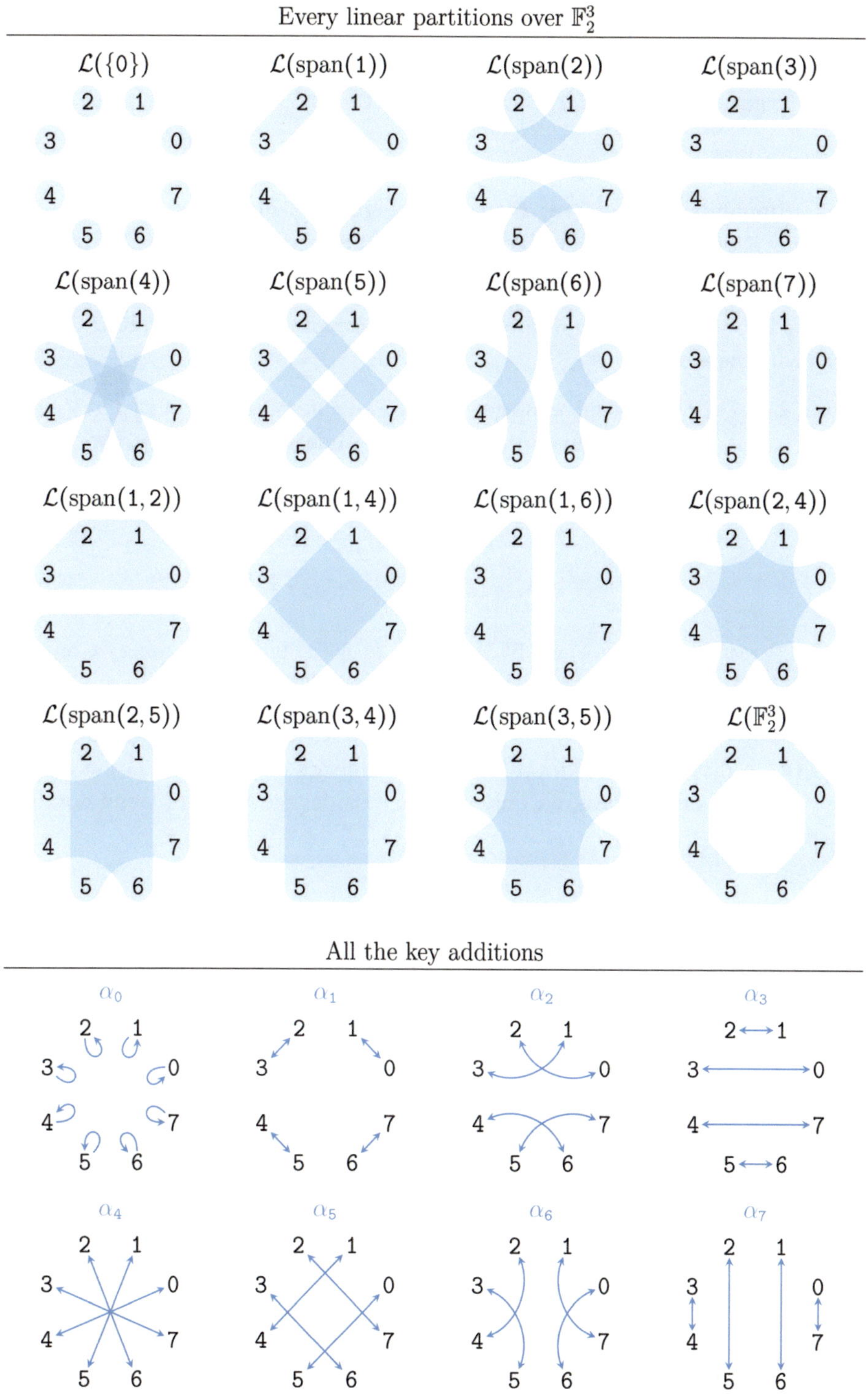

Figure 2.3. Every linear partitions and key addition in $\mathbb{F}_2^3$.

All the key additions are given at the bottom of **Figure 2.3.** The reverse implication of Proposition 2.13 states that any linear partition is preserved by all the key additions. For instance,

$$\begin{aligned}\alpha_2(\mathcal{L}(\text{span}(6)) &= \{f(\{0,6\}), f(\{1,7\}), f(\{2,4\}), f(\{3,5\})\} \\ &= \{\ \ \{2,4\},\quad \{3,5\},\quad \{0,6\},\quad \{1,7\}\ \ \} = \mathcal{L}(\text{span}(6)).\end{aligned}$$

Thus, the permutation α_2 preserves $\mathcal{L}(\text{span}(6))$. **Figure 2.4** illustrates graphically that this linear partition is preserved by all the key additions. It is then not hard to check that the same holds for every linear partition given in **Figure 2.3.** ▲

Now that we know linear partitions are of major importance, we focus on how the diffusion layer deals with these partitions.

Proposition 2.15. Let n be a positive integer. Let L be an automorphism of $\mathbb{F}_2^n$ and V a subspace of $\mathbb{F}_2^n$. Then, $L(\mathcal{L}(V)) = \mathcal{L}(L(V))$. In particular, L maps a linear partition to another one.

Proof. Since L is an automorphism, we have

$$\begin{aligned}L(\mathcal{L}(V)) &= L(\{x + V | x \in \mathbb{F}_2^n\}) = \{L(x + V) | x \in \mathbb{F}_2^n\} \\ &= \{L(x) + L(V) | x \in \mathbb{F}_2^n\} = \{x' + L(V) | x' \in \mathbb{F}_2^n\}.\end{aligned}$$

Moreover, $L(V)$ is a subspace of $\mathbb{F}_2^n$ because L is a linear mapping. Consequently, $L(\mathcal{L}(V)) = \mathcal{L}(L(V))$. ▪

If V and W are two subspaces of $\mathbb{F}_2^n$, it is straightforward to design a linear permutation L of $\mathbb{F}_2^n$ mapping $\mathcal{L}(V)$ to $\mathcal{L}(W)$. Indeed, Proposition 2.15 establishes that L maps $\mathcal{L}(V)$ to $\mathcal{L}(W)$ is and only if $L(V) = W$. In other words, we only need to consider the image of V and not the whole linear partition $\mathcal{L}(V)$.

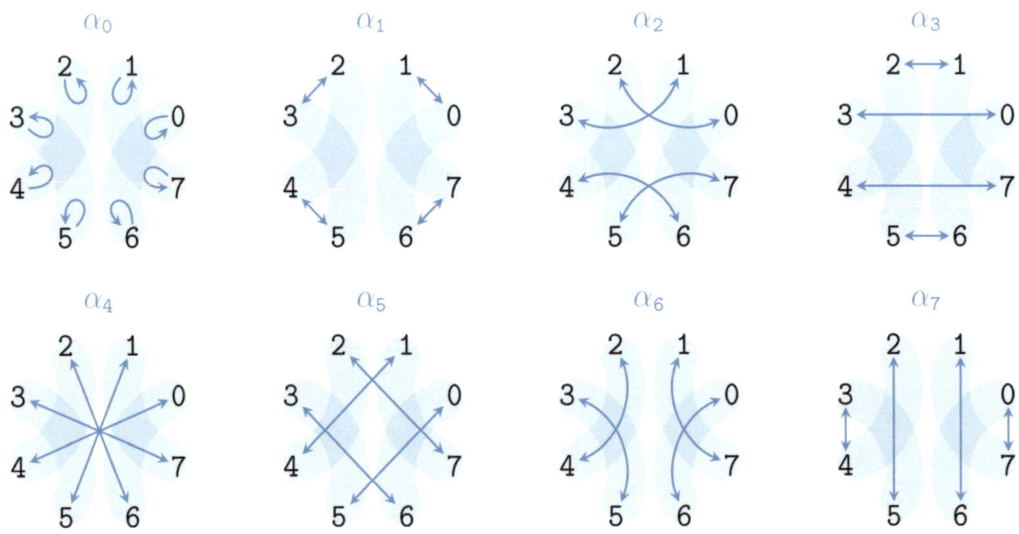

Figure 2.4. The key additions preserving the partition $\mathcal{L}(\text{span}(6))$.

2.2. From the encryption function to the substitution layer

Along with the two results of the previous section, we can now address our main issue. For the rest of this chapter, we consider a generic SPN whose parameters are defined as follows.

Definition 2.16 (SPN). Let m, n and r be positive integers. A *substitution-permutation network* is an iterated block cipher whose encryption function is defined as follows. Let $S_0,\ldots,S_{m-1}$ be n-bit S-boxes.

- The *addition* of the round key k is denoted by $\alpha_k : \mathbb{F}_2^{nm} \to \mathbb{F}_2^{nm}, x \mapsto x + k$.
- The *substitution layer* is denoted by σ and maps $(x_i)_{0\le i<m}$ to $(S_i(x_i))_{0\le i<m}$.
- The *diffusion layer* is a linear permutation denoted by $\pi : \mathbb{F}_2^{nm} \to \mathbb{F}_2^{nm}$.

The round function F_k associated with the round key k is defined by $F_k = \pi\sigma\alpha_k$. The *encryption function* associated with the round keys $K = (k^{[0]}, \ldots, k^{[r]})$ in $(\mathbb{F}_2^{nm})^{r+1}$ is defined by

$$E_K = \alpha_{k^{[r]}} F_{k^{[r-1]}} \ldots F_{k^{[0]}} .$$

We can now prove the following result.

Theorem 2.17. Let $\mathcal{A}$ and $\mathcal{B}$ be two partitions of $\mathbb{F}_2^{nm}$. Suppose for any $(r + 1)$-tuples of round keys $K = (k^{[0]}, \ldots, k^{[r]})$ in $(\mathbb{F}_2^{nm})^{r+1}$ that the encryption function E_K maps $\mathcal{A}$ to $\mathcal{B}$. Define $\mathcal{A}^{[0]} = \mathcal{A}$ and for all $1\le i\le r$, $\mathcal{A}^{[i]} = (\pi\sigma)^i(\mathcal{A})$. Then,

- $\mathcal{A}^{[r]} = \mathcal{B}$;
- for any $0 \le i < r$ and for any $k^{[i]}$ in $\mathbb{F}_2^{nm}$, $F_{k^{[i]}}(\mathcal{A}^{[i]}) = \mathcal{A}^{[i+1]}$;
- for any $0\le i\le r$, $\mathcal{A}^{[i]}$ is a linear partition.

Proof. Observe that for the round key $k = 0_{nm}$, the key addition $\alpha_{0_{nm}}$ is the identity mapping on $\mathbb{F}_2^{nm}$, and thus $F_{0_{nm}} = \pi\sigma\alpha_{0_{nm}} = \pi\sigma$. Now, choosing $K = (k^{[0]}, \ldots, k^{[r]}) = (0_{nm}, \ldots, 0_{nm})$ gives

$$\begin{aligned}\mathcal{B} = E_K(\mathcal{A}^{[0]}) &= \alpha_{k^{[r]}} F_{k^{[r-1]}} \ldots F_{k^{[0]}}(\mathcal{A}^{[0]}) = \alpha_{0_{nm}}(F_{0_{nm}})^r(\mathcal{A}^{[0]})\\ &= (\pi\sigma)^r(\mathcal{A}^{[0]}) = \mathcal{A}^{[r]}.\end{aligned}$$

Let $0 \le i < r$ be an integer. Let $k^{[i]}$ be any element of $\mathbb{F}_2^{nm}$. Define $k^{[j]} = 0_{nm}$ for all $0\le j\le r$ such that $j \ne i$. By hypothesis, the equality $\alpha_{k^{[r]}} F_{k^{[r-1]}} \ldots F_{k^{[0]}}(\mathcal{A}^{[0]}) = \mathcal{A}^{[r]}$ holds. Thus,

$$F_{k^{[i]}} \ldots F_{k^{[0]}}(\mathcal{A}^{[0]}) = (\alpha_{k^{[r]}} F_{k^{[r-1]}} \ldots F_{k^{[i+1]}})^{-1}(\mathcal{A}^{[r]}) .$$

On one hand,

$$\begin{aligned}F_{k^{[i]}} \ldots F_{k^{[0]}}(\mathcal{A}^{[0]}) &= F_{k^{[i]}}(F_{k^{[i-1]}} \ldots F_{k^{[0]}})(\mathcal{A}^{[0]}) = F_{k^{[i]}}(F_{0_{nm}})^i(\mathcal{A}^{[0]})\\ &= F_{k^{[i]}}(\pi\sigma)^i(\mathcal{A}^{[0]}) = F_{k^{[i]}}(\mathcal{A}^{[i]}).\end{aligned}$$

On the other hand,

$$\begin{aligned}(\alpha_{k^{[r]}}F_{k^{[r-1]}}\ldots F_{k^{[i+1]}})^{-1}(\mathcal{A}^{[r]}) &= (\alpha_{0_{nm}}(F_{0_{nm}})^{r-(i+1)})^{-1}(\mathcal{A}^{[r]})\\ &= ((\pi\sigma)^{r-(i+1)})^{-1}(\mathcal{A}^{[r]}) = \mathcal{A}^{[i+1]}.\end{aligned}$$

Therefore, $F_{k^{[i]}}(\mathcal{A}^{[i]}) = \mathcal{A}^{[i+1]}$, or equivalently $\alpha_{k^{[i]}}(\mathcal{A}^{[i]}) = (\pi\sigma)^{-1}(\mathcal{A}^{[i+1]})$. Since this equality holds for every $k^{[i]}$, Proposition 2.13 states that the partition $\mathcal{A}^{[i]}$ is linear.

It remains to show that $\mathcal{A}^{[r]}$ is linear as the previous argument holds only for $i < r$. Let $k^{[r]}$ be an element of $\mathbb{F}_2^{nm}$. Define $k^{[i]} = 0_{nm}$ for each $0 \leq i < r$. Then,

$$\mathcal{A}^{[r]} = \alpha_{k^{[r]}}F_{k^{[r-1]}}\ldots F_{k^{[0]}}(\mathcal{A}^{[0]}) = \alpha_{k^{[r]}}(F_{0_{nm}})^{r}(\mathcal{A}^{[0]}) = \alpha_{k^{[r]}}(\mathcal{A}^{[r]}).$$

Again, Proposition 2.13 implies that $\mathcal{A}^{[r]}$ is linear and the result is proven. ▪

This theorem can be restated in the following way. First, the input partition $\mathcal{A}$ and the output partition $\mathcal{B}$ must be linear. This result generalizes Proposition 2.13 in the sense that it applies to the full cipher and not only to the key addition. As was pointed out earlier, linear partitions are very specific partitions. This means that our combinatorial hypothesis implies to consider only algebraic objects.

Second, we have only supposed that the encryption function maps $\mathcal{A}$ to $\mathcal{B}$ after r rounds. Nevertheless, Theorem 2.17 ensures that each iteration of the round function also maps a fixed linear partition to another one. As a consequence, the study of the full cipher is reduced to the study of the round function. Additionally, this result can be strengthened as follows.

Corollary 2.18. Keep the notations of Theorem 2.17. For all $0 \leq i \leq r$, let $V^{[i]}$ denote the part of $\mathcal{A}^{[i]}$ containing 0. According to Theorem 2.17, $\mathcal{A}^{[i]} = \mathcal{L}(V^{[i]})$. Let $0 \leq i < r$ be an integer. Then,

$$\sigma(\mathcal{L}(V^{[i]})) = \mathcal{L}(W^{[i]}).$$

where $W^{[i]}$ denotes the subspace $\pi^{-1}(V^{[i+1]})$. In particular, the substitution layer must at least map one linear partition to another one.

Proof. By definition, $\pi\sigma(\mathcal{A}^{[i]}) = \mathcal{A}^{[i+1]}$ or, equivalently, $\sigma(\mathcal{A}^{[i]}) = \pi^{-1}(\mathcal{A}^{[i+1]})$. This equality can be restated as

$$\sigma(\mathcal{L}(V^{[i]})) = \pi^{-1}(\mathcal{L}(V^{[i+1]})).$$

As π is an automorphism of $\mathbb{F}_2^{nm}$, then so π^{-1} is. Next, Proposition 2.15 ensures that $\pi^{-1}(\mathcal{L}(V^{[i+1]})) = \mathcal{L}(\pi^{-1}(V^{[i+1]}))$. The result follows. ▪

A diagrammatic representation of Theorem 2.17 and Corollary 2.18 is given in **Figure 2.5.** This highlights that the input partition is always transformed in the same way through each basic operation of the encryption process. The results obtained so far can be summarized as follows: if an SPN maps a partition $\mathcal{A}$ of the plaintext space to a partition $\mathcal{B}$ of the ciphertext space no

http://dx.doi.org/10.5772/intechopen.70420

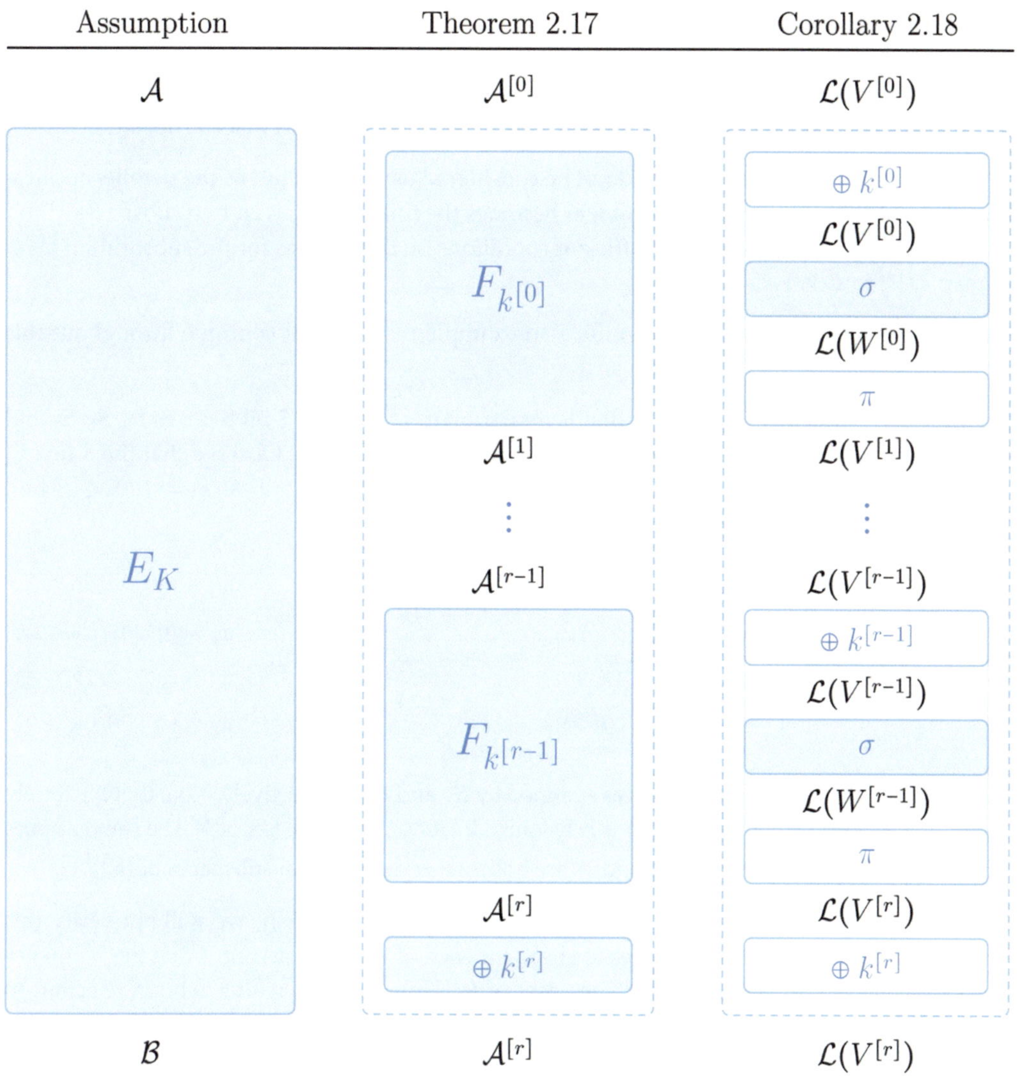

Figure 2.5. Results of Section 2.2.

matter the round keys used, then the substitution layer has to map at least one linear partition to another one. This shows that our study can be reduced to the substitution layer without loss of generality.

3. Structure of the substitution layer

In the remainder of this chapter, V and W will denote two subspaces of $(\mathbb{F}_2^n)^m$.

As explained in the previous section, it remains to understand how the substitution layer can map the linear partition $\mathcal{L}(V)$ to $\mathcal{L}(W)$. This problem is far more complex for the substitution layer than it was for the diffusion layer. The reasons for this are twofold. First, the substitution layer is nonlinear. It is even the only part of the SPN, which is not affine. As a consequence, to map the linear partition $\mathcal{L}(V)$ to $\mathcal{L}(W)$, we have to consider all the parts of both partitions and not only the subspaces V and W, as was the case for the diffusion layer (see Proposition 2.15).

Second, the substitution layer should not be considered as a whole, but as the parallel application of its S-boxes. Therefore our problem becomes the following. Given two subspaces V and W, what are the necessary and/or sufficient conditions on the S-boxes for the substitution layer to map $\mathcal{L}(V)$ to $\mathcal{L}(W)$.

Before going any further, let us introduce an example that we will continue throughout this section.

Example 2.19. Consider the substitution layer made up of the four 5-bit S-boxes S_0, S_1, S_2 and S_3 described in **Figure 2.6.** Its parameters are then $m = 4$ and $n = 5$. Observe that the S-box S_2 was previously studied in Example 2.7. Define the two families $\mathcal{E}_V = (v_i)_{0 \le i < 7}$ and $\mathcal{E}_W = (w_i)_{0 \le i < 7}$ of elements of $(\mathbb{F}_2^5)^4$ by

$$v_0 = (\mathtt{10}, \mathtt{00}, \mathtt{00}, \mathtt{17}), \quad v_1 = (\mathtt{08}, \mathtt{00}, \mathtt{00}, \mathtt{17}), \quad v_2 = (\mathtt{04}, \mathtt{00}, \mathtt{00}, \mathtt{0B}),$$

$$v_3 = (\mathtt{02}, \mathtt{00}, \mathtt{00}, \mathtt{1C}), \quad v_4 = (\mathtt{01}, \mathtt{00}, \mathtt{00}, \mathtt{1C}), \quad v_5 = (\mathtt{00}, \mathtt{00}, \mathtt{1A}, \mathtt{00}), \quad v_6 = (\mathtt{00}, \mathtt{00}, \mathtt{07}, \mathtt{00}).$$

$$w_0 = (\mathtt{10}, \mathtt{00}, \mathtt{00}, \mathtt{15}), \quad w_1 = (\mathtt{08}, \mathtt{00}, \mathtt{00}, \mathtt{1D}), \quad w_2 = (\mathtt{04}, \mathtt{00}, \mathtt{00}, \mathtt{15}),$$

$$w_3 = (\mathtt{02}, \mathtt{00}, \mathtt{00}, \mathtt{08}), \quad w_4 = (\mathtt{01}, \mathtt{00}, \mathtt{00}, \mathtt{00}), \quad w_5 = (\mathtt{00}, \mathtt{00}, \mathtt{12}, \mathtt{00}), \quad w_6 = (\mathtt{00}, \mathtt{00}, \mathtt{0E}, \mathtt{00}).$$

Finally, define V and W as the subspaces spanned by $\mathcal{E}_V$ and $\mathcal{E}_W$, respectively. Note that the family $\mathcal{E}_V$ is linearly independent because it is echelonized. Hence, $\mathcal{E}_V$ is a basis of V. The same applies for $\mathcal{E}_W$ and W. As a consequence, V and W are both seven-dimensional subspaces of $(\mathbb{F}_2^5)^4$.

We claim that the substitution layer σ maps $\mathcal{L}(V)$ to $\mathcal{L}(W)$. Naturally, we will not verify this statement by hand because it requires to check for each of the 2^{13} cosets of V that the 2^7 images of its elements under σ lies in the same coset of W. However, the reader who is relectant to accept this claim is encouraged to check it with a computer. ▲

		.0	.1	.2	.3	.4	.5	.6	.7	.8	.9	.A	.B	.C	.D	.E	.F
$S_0(x)$	0.	1F	19	03	05	1D	1B	01	07	14	12	1C	1A	16	10	1E	18
	1.	0E	08	09	0F	0C	0A	0B	0D	04	02	17	11	06	00	15	13
$S_1(x)$	0.	02	19	11	14	1B	0E	0C	07	15	0A	01	00	0D	1C	1D	12
	1.	06	1E	10	16	05	13	17	1F	18	04	09	0B	1A	08	0F	03
$S_2(x)$	0.	1E	08	04	13	0F	18	14	10	19	15	0E	0D	03	1C	07	17
	1.	12	11	0B	1B	09	05	1F	00	0A	01	02	1A	06	0C	1D	16
$S_3(x)$	0.	03	0A	10	1A	15	04	1C	0E	12	18	02	0B	06	14	0C	1D
	1.	1B	09	11	00	0F	05	1F	16	08	19	01	13	1E	17	0D	07

Figure 2.6. Specification of the S-boxes used throughout Section 3.

3.1. Truncating the substitution layer

To understand how the substitution layer can map $\mathcal{L}(V)$ to $\mathcal{L}(W)$, we will adopt a *divide and conquer* strategy. That is to say, we want to break down this problem into several independent sub-problems, each involving less S-boxes than the full substitution layer. The first idea is to truncate the substitution layer and the subspaces V and W to get a local view of what happens on some S-boxes.

Definition 2.20 (truncation and substitution layer). Let E be any non-empty subset of $[\![0,m[\![$ and define the following mappings

$$\begin{aligned} \mathrm{T}_E : (\mathbb{F}_2^n)^m &\to (\mathbb{F}_2^n)^E & \qquad \sigma_E : (\mathbb{F}_2^n)^E &\to (\mathbb{F}_2^n)^E \\ (x_i)_{0\leq i<m} &\mapsto (x_i)_{i\in E} & (x_i)_{i\in E} &\mapsto (S_i(x_i))_{i\in E}\,. \end{aligned}$$

If E has cardinality p, then we identify $(\mathbb{F}_2^n)^E$ with $(\mathbb{F}_2^n)^p$.

The mapping T_E allows to shorten a vector of $(\mathbb{F}_2^n)^m$ to keep only the coordinates whose indices belong to E. The application σ_E is a substitution layer truncated to the S-boxes whose indices lie in E.

Remark 2.21. Note that T_E is a linear mapping. Observe that $\sigma_{[\![0,m[\![}$ is the substitution layer of the SPN. Moreover, the truncated substitution layer $\sigma_{\{i\}}$ and the S-box S_i are equal for all $0\leq i < m$.

Proposition 2.22 (truncating to a few S-boxes). Suppose that σ maps $\mathcal{L}(V)$ to $\mathcal{L}(W)$. Let E be a nonempty subset of $[\![0,m[\![$. Then, the permutation σ_E maps $\mathcal{L}(\mathrm{T}_E(V))$ to $\mathcal{L}(\mathrm{T}_E(W))$.

Proof. Let $x = (x_i)_{i\in E}$ be an element of $(\mathbb{F}_2^n)^E$. Let y be the element of $(\mathbb{F}_2^n)^m$ defined by $y_i = x_i$ if i belongs to E and $y_i = 0_n$ otherwise. Thus, $\mathrm{T}_E(y) = x$. By hypothesis, σ maps $\mathcal{L}(V)$ to $\mathcal{L}(W)$. Hence, Lemma 2.8 implies that $\sigma(y + V) = \sigma(y) + W$. Next,

$$\mathrm{T}_E(\sigma(y + V)) = \mathrm{T}_E(\sigma(y)) + \mathrm{T}_E(W)$$

since T_E is a linear mapping. Furthermore,

$$\begin{aligned} \mathrm{T}_E(\sigma(y + V)) &= \mathrm{T}_E\sigma(\{y + v|v\in V\}) = \{\mathrm{T}_E\sigma(y + v)|v\in V\} \\ &= \{\sigma_E(\mathrm{T}_E(y + v))|v\in V\} = \sigma_E(\{\mathrm{T}_E(y + v)|v\in V\}) \\ &= \sigma_E(\{\mathrm{T}_E(y) + \mathrm{T}_E(v)|v\in V\}) = \sigma_E(\mathrm{T}_E(y) + \mathrm{T}_E(V))\,. \end{aligned}$$

Therefore, $\sigma_E(x + \mathrm{T}_E(V)) = \mathrm{T}_E(\sigma(y)) + \mathrm{T}_E(W)$. In other words, the image of any part of $\mathcal{L}(\mathrm{T}_E(V))$ under σ_E lies in $\mathcal{L}(\mathrm{T}_E(W))$. The result is a consequence of Lemma 2.4. ▪

Example 2.23. By choosing $E = \{0, 3\}$, the previous proposition ensures that the truncated substitution layer $\sigma_{\{0,3\}}$ maps $\mathcal{L}(\mathrm{T}_{\{0,3\}}(V))$ to $\mathcal{L}(\mathrm{T}_{\{0,3\}}(W))$. First, it is easy to see that

$$\begin{aligned} \mathrm{T}_{\{0,3\}}(V) &= \mathrm{span}((\mathtt{10}, \mathtt{17}), (\mathtt{08}, \mathtt{17}), (\mathtt{04}, \mathtt{0B}), (\mathtt{02}, \mathtt{1C}), (\mathtt{01}, \mathtt{1C})), \\ \mathrm{T}_{\{0,3\}}(W) &= \mathrm{span}((\mathtt{10}, \mathtt{15}), (\mathtt{08}, \mathtt{1D}), (\mathtt{04}, \mathtt{15}), (\mathtt{02}, \mathtt{08}), (\mathtt{01}, \mathtt{00})). \end{aligned}$$

Again, we will not explicitly check that $\sigma_{\{0,3\}}$ maps $\mathcal{L}(\mathrm{T}_{\{0,3\}}(V))$ to $\mathcal{L}(\mathrm{T}_{\{0,3\}}(W))$ but limit ourselves to prove that the coset $(\texttt{07},\texttt{03})+\mathrm{T}_{\{0,3\}}(V)$ is mapped to one coset of $\mathrm{T}_{\{0,3\}}(W)$. Its image can be found using Lemma 2.8 as follow

$$\begin{aligned}\sigma_{\{0,3\}}((\texttt{07},\texttt{03})+\mathrm{T}_{\{0,3\}}(V)) &= \sigma_{\{0,3\}}((\texttt{07},\texttt{03}))+\mathrm{T}_{\{0,3\}}(W)\\ &= (\texttt{07},\texttt{1A})+\mathrm{T}_{\{0,3\}}(W)\,.\end{aligned}$$

The images of every element of this coset are given in **Figure 2.7.** For instance,

$$\begin{aligned}\sigma_{\{0,3\}}((\texttt{07},\texttt{03})+(\texttt{01},\texttt{1C})) = \sigma_{\{0,3\}}(\texttt{06},\texttt{1F}) &= (S_0(\texttt{06}),S_3(\texttt{1F})) = (\texttt{01},\texttt{07})\\ &= (\texttt{07},\texttt{1A})+(\texttt{06},\texttt{1D})\,.\end{aligned}$$

This explains the second image. ▲

Choosing $E=\{i\}$ in Proposition 2.22 gives that the S-box S_i maps $\mathcal{L}(\mathrm{T}_{\{i\}}(V))$ to $\mathcal{L}(\mathrm{T}_{\{i\}}(W))$. As this result holds for each index i in $[\![0,m[\![$, we deduce that

$$\sigma(\mathcal{L}(V))=\mathcal{L}(W) \quad\Rightarrow\quad \forall i\in[\![0,m[\![,\ S_i(\mathcal{L}(\mathrm{T}_{\{i\}}(V)))=\mathcal{L}(\mathrm{T}_{\{i\}}(W))\,. \tag{2.1}$$

However, the equivalence does not hold in general. Hence, this only gives a necessary condition on each S-box. In other words, this means that we can lose information when considering each S-box independently. The next example stresses this fact.

Example 2.24. In our example, the truncated subspaces $\mathrm{T}_{\{i\}}(V)$ and $\mathrm{T}_{\{i\}}(W)$ are the following:

$$\begin{aligned}&\mathrm{T}_{\{0\}}(V)=\mathbb{F}_2^5,\ \mathrm{T}_{\{1\}}(V)=\{\texttt{00}\},\ \mathrm{T}_{\{2\}}(V)=\mathrm{span}(\texttt{07},\texttt{1A}),\ \mathrm{T}_{\{3\}}(V)=\mathrm{span}(\texttt{0B},\texttt{17}),\\ &\mathrm{T}_{\{0\}}(W)=\mathbb{F}_2^5,\ \mathrm{T}_{\{1\}}(W)=\{\texttt{00}\},\ \mathrm{T}_{\{2\}}(W)=\mathrm{span}(\texttt{0B},\texttt{17}),\ \mathrm{T}_{\{3\}}(W)=\mathrm{span}(\texttt{08},\texttt{15}).\end{aligned}$$

$(07,03)+\mathrm{T}_{\{0,3\}}(V)$	$\longrightarrow$	$(07,1A)+\mathrm{T}_{\{0,3\}}(W)$	$(07,03)+\mathrm{T}_{\{0,3\}}(V)$	$\longrightarrow$	$(07,1A)+\mathrm{T}_{\{0,3\}}(W)$
(07,03) + (00,00)	⟼	(07,1A) + (00,00)	(07,03) + (10,17)	⟼	(07,1A) + (0A,15)
(07,03) + (01,1C)	⟼	(07,1A) + (06,1D)	(07,03) + (11,0B)	⟼	(07,1A) + (0C,08)
(07,03) + (02,1C)	⟼	(07,1A) + (1C,1D)	(07,03) + (12,0B)	⟼	(07,1A) + (0D,08)
(07,03) + (03,00)	⟼	(07,1A) + (1A,00)	(07,03) + (13,17)	⟼	(07,1A) + (0B,15)
(07,03) + (04,0B)	⟼	(07,1A) + (02,08)	(07,03) + (14,1C)	⟼	(07,1A) + (08,1D)
(07,03) + (05,17)	⟼	(07,1A) + (04,15)	(07,03) + (15,00)	⟼	(07,1A) + (0E,00)
(07,03) + (06,17)	⟼	(07,1A) + (1E,15)	(07,03) + (16,00)	⟼	(07,1A) + (0F,00)
(07,03) + (07,0B)	⟼	(07,1A) + (18,08)	(07,03) + (17,1C)	⟼	(07,1A) + (09,1D)
(07,03) + (08,17)	⟼	(07,1A) + (1F,15)	(07,03) + (18,00)	⟼	(07,1A) + (14,00)
(07,03) + (09,0B)	⟼	(07,1A) + (19,08)	(07,03) + (19,1C)	⟼	(07,1A) + (12,1D)
(07,03) + (0A,0B)	⟼	(07,1A) + (17,08)	(07,03) + (1A,1C)	⟼	(07,1A) + (07,1D)
(07,03) + (0B,17)	⟼	(07,1A) + (11,15)	(07,03) + (1B,00)	⟼	(07,1A) + (01,00)
(07,03) + (0C,1C)	⟼	(07,1A) + (1D,1D)	(07,03) + (1C,0B)	⟼	(07,1A) + (16,08)
(07,03) + (0D,00)	⟼	(07,1A) + (1B,00)	(07,03) + (1D,17)	⟼	(07,1A) + (10,15)
(07,03) + (0E,00)	⟼	(07,1A) + (15,00)	(07,03) + (1E,17)	⟼	(07,1A) + (05,15)
(07,03) + (0F,1C)	⟼	(07,1A) + (13,1D)	(07,03) + (1F,0B)	⟼	(07,1A) + (03,08)

Figure 2.7. $\sigma_{\{0,3\}}$ mapping a coset of $\mathrm{T}_{\{0,3\}}(V)$ to a coset of $\mathrm{T}_{\{0,3\}}(W)$.

First, observe that the truncated subspaces for S_0 and S_1 are trivial. Hence, the associated linear partitions are also trivial and no information on S_0 or S_1 can be drawn from 2.1. Yet, the last two truncated subspaces are nontrivial and 1 gives the following equalities:

$$S_2(\mathcal{L}(\text{span}(\texttt{07}, \texttt{1A}))) = \mathcal{L}(\text{span}(\texttt{0B}, \texttt{17})),$$
$$S_3(\mathcal{L}(\text{span}(\texttt{0B}, \texttt{17}))) = \mathcal{L}(\text{span}(\texttt{08}, \texttt{15})).$$

The first property has already been highlighted in Example 2.7 and in **Figure 2.2.** The second one is represented in **Figure 2.8.**

Let us now show that the converse of Implication 2.1 does not hold in general. Consider the substitution layer σ' made up of the four S-boxes S'_0, S'_1, S'_2 and S'_3 where

$$S'_0 = S_1, \quad S'_1 = S_1, \quad S'_2 = S_2, \quad S'_3 = S_3.$$

Thus, this new substitution layer differs from σ by only one S-box. Recall that the linear partition associated with $T_{\{0\}}(V) = T_{\{0\}}(W)$ is trivial. Therefore, S'_0 necessarily preserves this partition. As the other S-boxes remain the same, the right side of 2.1 still holds for σ', that is

$$\forall i \in [\![0,4[\![, S'_i(\mathcal{L}(T_{\{i\}}(V))) = \mathcal{L}(T_{\{i\}}(W)).$$

However, we will prove that σ' does not map $\mathcal{L}(V)$ to $\mathcal{L}(W)$. Suppose by contradiction that it does. Then Proposition 2.22 ensures that $\sigma'_{\{0,3\}}$ maps $\mathcal{L}(T_{\{0,3\}}(V))$ to $\mathcal{L}(T_{\{0,3\}}(W))$. By Lemma 2.8,

$$\begin{aligned}\sigma'_{\{0,3\}}((\texttt{07},\texttt{03}) + T_{\{0,3\}}(V)) &= \sigma'_{\{0,3\}}(\texttt{07},\texttt{03}) + T_{\{0,3\}}(W) \\ &= (S'_0(\texttt{07}), S'_3(\texttt{03})) + T_{\{0,3\}}(W) \\ &= (S_1(\texttt{07}), S_3(\texttt{03})) + T_{\{0,3\}}(W) = (\texttt{07},\texttt{1A}) + T_{\{0,3\}}(W).\end{aligned}$$

Then

$$\begin{aligned}\sigma'_{\{0,3\}}((\texttt{07},\texttt{03}) + (\texttt{01},\texttt{1C})) &= \sigma'_{\{0,3\}}(\texttt{06},\texttt{1F}) = (S'_0(\texttt{06}), S'_3(\texttt{1F})) = (S_1(\texttt{06}), S_3(\texttt{1F})) \\ &= (\texttt{0C},\texttt{07}) = (\texttt{07},\texttt{1A}) + (\texttt{0B},\texttt{1D}).\end{aligned}$$

This is a contradiction since (0B,1D) does not belong to T $_{\{0,3\}}(W)$ as can be seen in **Figure 2.7.** As a consequence, the substitution layer σ' does not map $\mathcal{L}(V)$ to $\mathcal{L}(W)$. ▲

As shown in the previous example, truncating the substitution layer and the subspaces V and W to each S-box independently of the others is too restrictive in general. This suggests that

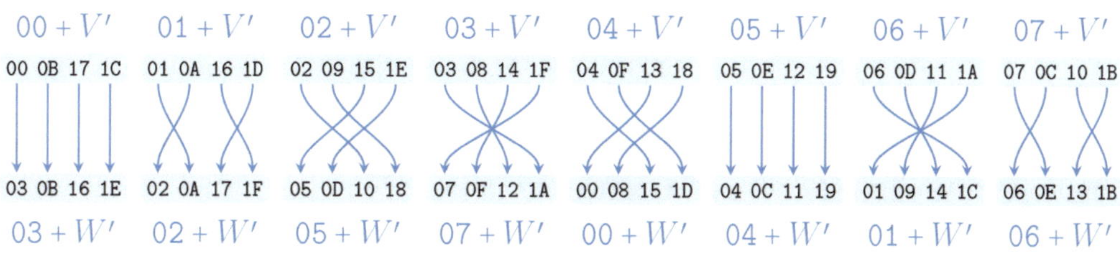

Figure 2.8. The S-box S_3 mapping $\mathcal{L}(V')$ to $\mathcal{L}(W')$ where $V' = \text{span}(\texttt{0B}, \texttt{17})$ and $W' = \text{span}(\texttt{08}, \texttt{15})$.

some S-boxes can in a way be linked together. That is to say, considering them independently results in a loss of information on the subspaces V and W. Recall that we are interested in splitting the problem of finding all the substitution layers σ mapping $\mathcal{L}(V)$ to $\mathcal{L}(W)$ into several independent smaller problems. Taking into account that some S-boxes can be linked together, we require the following:

- a sub-problem can involve several S-boxes;
- the same S-box cannot be involved in two different sub-problems (in other words, the sub-problems are independent);
- each S-box is involved in one sub-problem (possibly trivial).

This is naturally formalized by a partition $\mathcal{I}$ of $[\![0,m[\![$. Each part I of $\mathcal{I}$ represents a sub-problem, and its elements are the indices of the S-boxes involved in. By virtue of Proposition 2.22, it holds that

$$\sigma(\mathcal{L}(V)) = \mathcal{L}(W) \quad \Rightarrow \quad \forall I \in \mathcal{I}, \sigma_I(\mathcal{L}(\mathrm{T}_I(V))) = \mathcal{L}(\mathrm{T}_I(W)) \,. \tag{2.2}$$

The next section aims to find a sufficient condition on the partition $\mathcal{I}$ to obtain the equivalence. In such a case, this means that combining the solutions of these sub-problems yields a substitution layer mapping $\mathcal{L}(V)$ to $\mathcal{L}(W)$ and vice versa.

3.2. Structure of the subspaces V and W

With the aim of ending up with partitions for which the converse of 2.2 holds, let us introduce a few definitions and notations.

Definition 2.25 (trivial product). Let E be a subset of $[\![0,m[\![$. The *trivial product subspace* associated with E, denoted by Triv_E, is defined to be

$$\mathrm{Triv}_E = \{x \in (\mathbb{F}_2^n)^m \mid \forall i \in E^c, x_i = 0_n\} \,.$$

Moreover, we denote by V_E the intersection of V and Triv_E, that is $V_E = V \cap \mathrm{Triv}_E = \{v \in V \mid \forall i \in E^c, v_i = 0_n\}$. The subspace W_E is defined in the same way.

Remark 2.26. It is easily seen that

$$\mathrm{Triv}_E = \prod_{i=0}^{m-1} \mathrm{Triv}_E^{[i]} \quad \text{with} \quad \mathrm{Triv}_E^{[i]} = \begin{cases} \{0_n\} & \text{if } i \in E^c \,, \\ \mathbb{F}_2^n & \text{if } i \in E \,. \end{cases}$$

Thus, a trivial product subspace is the Cartesian product of trivial spaces for each S-box; this justifies its name. Additionally, if $E \subseteq F$, then $\mathrm{Triv}_E \subseteq \mathrm{Triv}_F$, and hence $V_E \subseteq V_F$ and $W_E \subseteq W_F$.

The subspaces Triv_E are essential in the study of the substitution layer because the latter always preserves the partition $\mathcal{L}(\mathrm{Triv}_E)$ regardless of its S-boxes. This result, together with Proposition 2.10, establishes the following corollary.

Corollary 2.27. Let E be a subset of $[\![0,m[\![$. If σ maps $\mathcal{L}(V)$ to $\mathcal{L}(W)$, then σ also maps $\mathcal{L}(V_E)$ to $\mathcal{L}(W_E)$.

Example 2.28. All the subspaces V_E are graphically represented in **Figure 2.9.** For instance,

$$V_{\{0\}} = \text{span}((\texttt{15}, \texttt{00}, \texttt{00}, \texttt{00}), (\texttt{0D}, \texttt{00}, \texttt{00}, \texttt{00}), (\texttt{03}, \texttt{00}, \texttt{00}, \texttt{00}))\,.$$

Additionally, this figure also highlights the expected inclusions given by Remark 2.26. Observe that $\mathcal{B}_V = (v_i)_{0\leq i<7}$ is a basis of V. This new basis is more convenient than the echelonized basis $\mathcal{E}_V$ previously introduced in Example 2.19 since all the V_E are then easily described. It is worth noting that the same picture remains valid for the subspace W. For example,

$$v_0 = (\texttt{15},\texttt{00},\texttt{00},\texttt{00}),\quad v_3 = (\texttt{04},\texttt{00},\texttt{00},\texttt{0B}),\qquad w_0 = (\texttt{14},\texttt{00},\texttt{00},\texttt{00}),\quad w_3 = (\texttt{04},\texttt{00},\texttt{00},\texttt{15}),$$
$$v_1 = (\texttt{0D},\texttt{00},\texttt{00},\texttt{00}),\quad v_4 = (\texttt{01},\texttt{00},\texttt{00},\texttt{1C}),\qquad w_1 = (\texttt{0E},\texttt{00},\texttt{00},\texttt{00}),\quad w_4 = (\texttt{02},\texttt{00},\texttt{00},\texttt{08}),$$
$$v_2 = (\texttt{03},\texttt{00},\texttt{00},\texttt{00}),\quad v_5 = (\texttt{00},\texttt{00},\texttt{1A},\texttt{00}),\qquad w_2 = (\texttt{01},\texttt{00},\texttt{00},\texttt{00}),\quad w_5 = (\texttt{00},\texttt{00},\texttt{12},\texttt{00}),$$
$$v_6 = (\texttt{00},\texttt{00},\texttt{07},\texttt{00}).\qquad w_6 = (\texttt{00},\texttt{00},\texttt{0E},\texttt{00}).$$

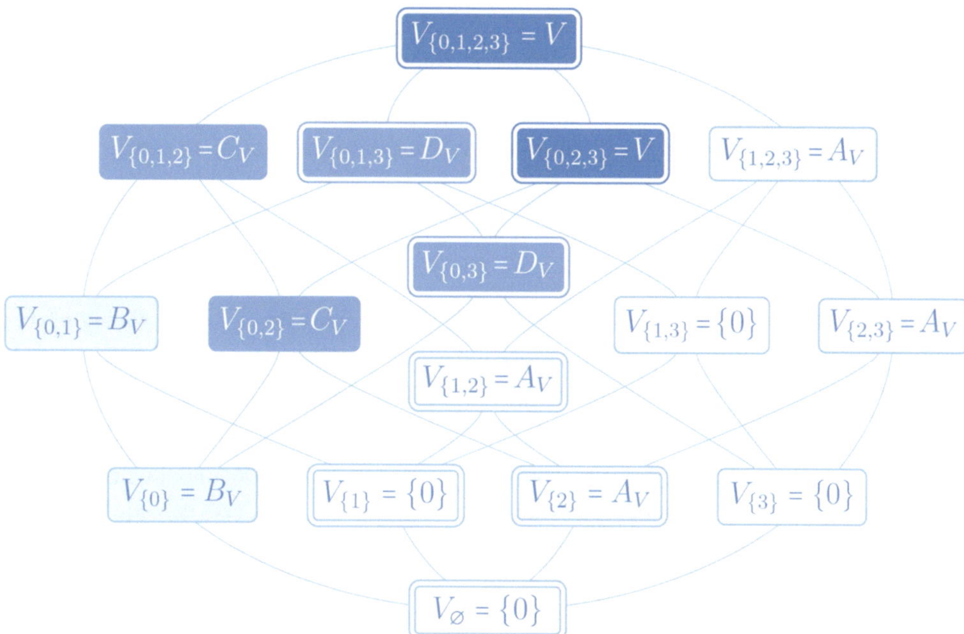

$$A_V = \text{span}(v_5, v_6),\qquad A_W = \text{span}(w_5, w_6),$$
$$B_V = \text{span}(v_0, v_1, v_2),\qquad B_W = \text{span}(w_0, w_1, w_2),$$
$$C_V = \text{span}(v_0, v_1, v_2, v_3, v_4),\qquad C_W = \text{span}(w_0, w_1, w_2, w_3, w_4),$$
$$D_V = \text{span}(v_0, v_1, v_2, v_5, v_6).\qquad D_W = \text{span}(w_0, w_1, w_2, w_5, w_6).$$

Figure 2.9. The subspaces V_E, W_E for each subset E of {0,1,2,3}.

$$W_{\{0\}} = \text{span}((\texttt{14}, \texttt{00}, \texttt{00}, \texttt{00}), (\texttt{0E}, \texttt{00}, \texttt{00}, \texttt{00}), (\texttt{01}, \texttt{00}, \texttt{00}, \texttt{00}))\,.$$

This emphasizes that when the substitution layer maps $\mathcal{L}(V)$ to $\mathcal{L}(W)$, the subspaces V and W have the same structure.

According to Corollary 2.27, the substitution layer maps $\mathcal{L}(V_{\{0\}})$ to $\mathcal{L}(W_{\{0\}})$. Next, truncate to $E = \{0\}$ using Proposition 2.22 to obtain

$$S_0(\mathcal{L}(\text{span}(\texttt{03}, \texttt{0D}, \texttt{15}))) = \mathcal{L}(\text{span}(\texttt{01}, \texttt{0E}, \texttt{14}))\,.$$

This property is depicted in **Figure 2.10.** Finally, it should be underlined that with Proposition 2.22 alone, no property can be established on the S-box S_0 (see Example 2.24). ▲

Definition 2.29 (projection P_E). Let E be a subset of $[\![0,m[\![$. The *projection* P_E from $(\mathbb{F}_2^n)^m$ onto Triv_E is defined by $\mathrm{P}_E(x_0, \ldots, x_{m-1}) = (y_0, \ldots, y_{m-1})$ where $y_i = x_i$ if i belongs to E and $y_i = 0_n$ otherwise.

Remark 2.30. It is not hard to see that P_E is a linear mapping and that V_E is always a subspace of $\mathrm{P}_E(V)$. Moreover, it holds that $\mathrm{T}_E(V) = \mathrm{T}_E(\mathrm{P}_E(V))$.

The next lemma gives some relations between the previous definitions. It is quite important and will be used several times by the end of the current chapter.

Lemma 2.31. Let $\mathcal{I}$ be a partition of $[\![0,m[\![$. Then V equals the internal direct sum $\bigoplus_{I\in\mathcal{I}} V_I$ if and only if $V_I = \mathrm{P}_I(V)$ for any part I of $\mathcal{I}$. In this case, the decomposition of an element v of V is $v = \sum_{I\in\mathcal{I}} \mathrm{P}_I(v)$.

Remark 2.32. Suppose that $\mathcal{I}$ is a partition of $[\![0,m[\![$ such that $V = \bigoplus_{I\in\mathcal{I}} V_I$. The previous lemma, together with Remark 2.30, establishes that $\mathrm{T}_I(V) = \mathrm{T}_I(V_I)$ for each part I of $\mathcal{I}$.

Proposition 2.33 (Substitution layer structure). Let $\mathcal{I}$ be a partition of $[\![0,m[\![$ satisfying both $V = \bigoplus_{I\in\mathcal{I}} V_I$ and $W = \bigoplus_{I\in\mathcal{I}} W_I$. The permutation σ maps $\mathcal{L}(V)$ to $\mathcal{L}(W)$ if and only if σ_I maps $\mathcal{L}(\mathrm{T}_I(V))$ to $\mathcal{L}(\mathrm{T}_I(W))$ for any I in $\mathcal{I}$.

The preceding proposition establishes that the converse of Implication 2.2 (page 21) holds whenever the partition $\mathcal{I}$ satisfies both $V = \bigoplus_{I\in\mathcal{I}} V_I$ and $W = \bigoplus_{I\in\mathcal{I}} W_I$. For such a partition, the problem of finding all the substitution layers σ mapping $\mathcal{L}(V)$ to $\mathcal{L}(W)$ can equivalently be broken down into the independent sub-problems of finding all the σ_I mapping $\mathcal{L}(\mathrm{T}_I(V))$ to $\mathcal{L}(\mathrm{T}_I(W))$ for each part I of $\mathcal{I}$.

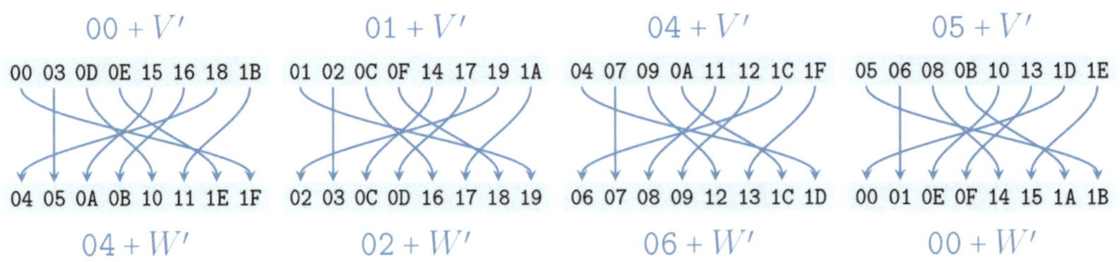

Figure 2.10. The S-box S_0 mapping $\mathcal{L}(V')$ to $\mathcal{L}(W')$ where $V' = \text{span}(\texttt{03}, \texttt{0D}, \texttt{15})$ and $W' = \text{span}(\texttt{01}, \texttt{0E}, \texttt{14})$.

3.3. Linked and independent S-boxes

Of course, there may be several partitions $\mathcal{I}$ such that $V = \bigoplus_{I\in\mathcal{I}} V_I$ and $W = \bigoplus_{I\in\mathcal{I}} W_I$, each yielding a different decomposition of the substitution layer. A few of these decompositions are certainly more interesting or easier to solve. The purpose of this section is to study such partitions. Let us begin with the following lemma.

Lemma 2.34. Suppose that σ maps $\mathcal{L}(V)$ to $\mathcal{L}(W)$. For every partition $\mathcal{I}$ of $[\![0,m[\![$, $V = \bigoplus_{I\in\mathcal{I}} V_I$ if and only if $W = \bigoplus_{I\in\mathcal{I}} W_I$.

The contrapositive of Lemma 2.34 is the following: if there exists a partition $\mathcal{I}$ such that $V = \bigoplus_{I\in\mathcal{I}} V_I$ and $W \neq \bigoplus_{I\in\mathcal{I}} W_I$ or such that $V \neq \bigoplus_{I\in\mathcal{I}} V_I$ and $W = \bigoplus_{I\in\mathcal{I}} W_I$, then there exists no substitution layer mapping $\mathcal{L}(V)$ to $\mathcal{L}(W)$. Because we intend to study the substitution layers mapping $\mathcal{L}(V)$ to $\mathcal{L}(W)$, Lemma 2.34 suggests to assume the following.

Assumption 2.35. For the remainder of this section, we assume that for any partition $\mathcal{I}$ of $[\![0,m[\![$, it holds that

$$V = \bigoplus_{I\in\mathcal{I}} V_I \Leftrightarrow W = \bigoplus_{I\in\mathcal{I}} W_I .$$

Proposition 2.33, together with the preceding assumption, suggests the following definition.

Definition 2.36 (decomposition partition). A *decomposition partition* (with respect to V and W) is a partition of $[\![0,m[\![$ such that $V = \bigoplus_{I\in\mathcal{I}} V_I$.

Remark 2.37 (partial order on partitions). Recall that if $\mathcal{I}$ and $\mathcal{J}$ are two partitions of $[\![0,m[\![$, then the partition $\mathcal{I}$ is said to be *finer* than $\mathcal{J}$ if for any part I in $\mathcal{I}$, there exists a part J in $\mathcal{J}$ such that $I \subseteq J$.

Example 2.38. The purpose of this example is to find all the decomposition partitions with regard to V and W. By virtue of Lemma 2.31, the subspace V can be decomposed as $\bigoplus_{I\in\mathcal{I}} V_I$ if and only if V_I is equal to $\mathrm{P}_I(V)$ for each part I of $\mathcal{I}$. The eight-framed subspaces in the middle of **Figure 2.9** are exactly those that satisfy $V_E = \mathrm{P}_E(V)$. Hence, the decomposition partitions are the partitions whose parts are selected from the following:

$$\varnothing,\ \{1\},\ \{2\},\ \{1,2\},\ \{0,3\},\ \{0,1,3\},\ \{0,2,3\},\ \{0,1,2,3\}\,.$$

It is then easy to check that the decomposition partitions of V are:

$$\begin{array}{ccc} \{\{1\},\{2\},\{0,3\}\}, & \{\{1\},\{0,2,3\}\}, & \{\{2\},\{0,1,3\}\}, \\ \{\{0,3\},\{1,2\}\} & \text{and} & \{\{0,1,2,3\}\}\,. \end{array}$$

In **Figure 2.11**, all the partitions of $[\![0,4[\![$ are ordered by the *"finer-than"* relation, and the decomposition partitions are emphasized. What stands out is that the decomposition partition {{1}, {2}, {0, 3}} is finer than all other decomposition partitions. ▲

The existence of this least decomposition partition in the example above is a very welcome and nontrivial property. This means that all the truncated substitution layers obtained using

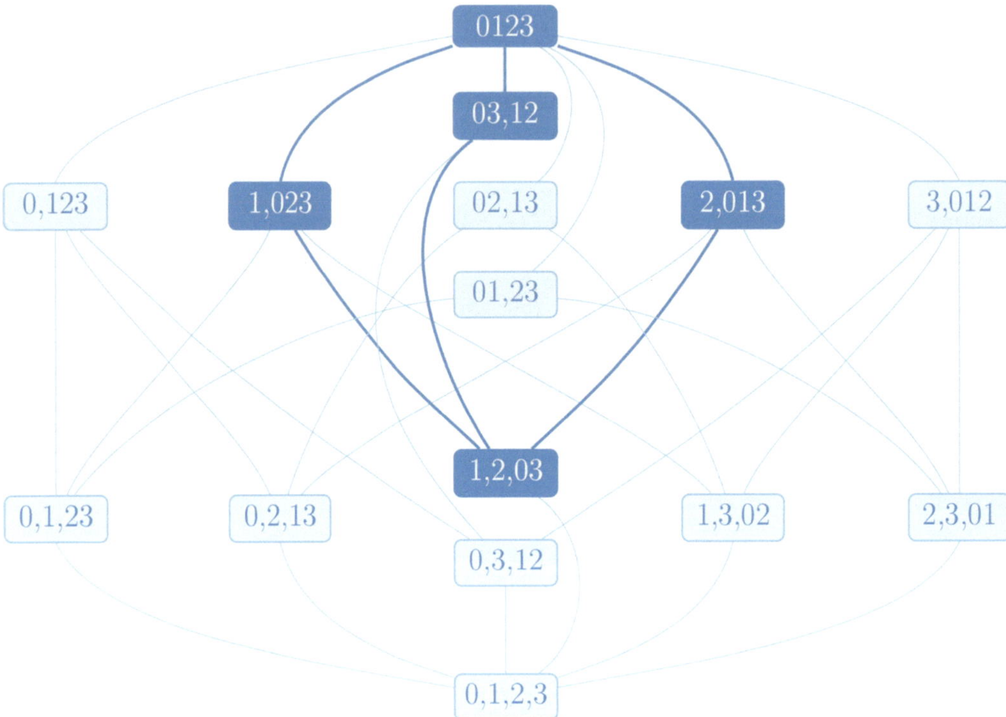

Figure 2.11. The partitions $\mathcal{I}$ of {0, 1, 2, 3} such that $V = \oplus_{I \in \mathcal{I}} V_I$.

Proposition 2.33 are the smallest possible. Thus, such a partition should be preferred to any other decomposition partition. We will now prove that this least decomposition partition always exists.

Proposition 2.39. The set of the partitions $\mathcal{I}$ of $[\![0,m[\![$ satisfying $V = \oplus_{I \in \mathcal{I}} V_I$ has a least element denoted $\mathcal{I}_{\text{ld}}$.

Consequently, the only decomposition partition that will be considered in the remainder of this chapter is the least decomposition partition $\mathcal{I}_{\text{ld}}$. The following definition is inspired by Proposition 2.33 and Proposition 2.39.

Definition 2.40 (linked and independent S-boxes). Suppose that σ maps $\mathcal{L}(V)$ to $\mathcal{L}(W)$. Let I be a part of $\mathcal{I}_{\text{ld}}$.

- If $I = \{i\}$, the S-box S_i is said to be *independent* of the other S-boxes.

  Moreover, if $V_{\{i\}} = \{0_{nm}\}$ or $V_{\{i\}} = \text{Triv}_{\{i\}}$, the S-box S_i is said to be *inactive*. Otherwise, S_i is *active*.

- If $\#I \geq 2$, then the S-boxes whose indices lie in I are said to be *linked together*.

Remark 2.41. Let $0 \leq i \leq m$ be an integer. We have already noted that the substitution layer σ always preserves $\mathcal{L}(\{0_{nm}\})$ and $\mathcal{L}(\text{Triv}_{\{i\}})$. In addition, Proposition 2.33 ensures that σ maps $\mathcal{L}(V_{\{i\}})$ to $\mathcal{L}(W_{\{i\}})$. Consequently, if $V_{\{i\}} = \{0_{nm}\}$ or if $V_{\{i\}} = \text{Triv}_{\{i\}}$, then $V_{\{i\}} = W_{\{i\}}$.

Suppose that the S-box S_i is independent with regard to the subspaces V and W. As established by Proposition 2.33 and Remark 2.32, if S_i is replaced with another S-box S'_i, then this new substitution layer still maps $\mathcal{L}(V)$ to $\mathcal{L}(W)$ provided that S'_i maps $\mathcal{L}(\mathrm{T}_{\{i\}}(V_{\{i\}}))$ to $\mathcal{L}(\mathrm{T}_{\{i\}}(W_{\{i\}}))$.

Suppose further that S_i is active. By definition, $\{0_{nm}\} \not\subseteq V_{\{i\}} \not\subseteq \mathrm{Triv}_{\{i\}}$. Observe that the restriction of $\mathrm{T}_{\{i\}}$ to $\mathrm{Triv}_{\{i\}}$ is one-to-one, hence

$$\{0_n\} = \mathrm{T}_{\{i\}}(\{0_{nm}\}) \not\subseteq \mathrm{T}_{\{i\}}(V_{\{i\}}) \not\subseteq \mathrm{T}_{\{i\}}(\mathrm{Triv}_{\{i\}}) = \mathbb{F}_2^n .$$

Thus, $\mathrm{T}_{\{i\}}(V_{\{i\}})$ is a nontrivial subspace of $\mathbb{F}_2^n$ and the requirement that S'_i maps $\mathcal{L}(\mathrm{T}_{\{i\}}(V_{\{i\}}))$ to $\mathcal{L}(\mathrm{T}_{\{i\}}(W_{\{i\}}))$ is also nontrivial. Therefore, an independent active S-box can be chosen independently of the other S-boxes but has to respect the structure of the subspaces V and W.

Now suppose that S_i is inactive. By definition, $V_{\{i\}} = \{0_{nm}\}$ or $V_{\{i\}} = \mathrm{Triv}_{\{i\}}$. Then, the equality $V_{\{i\}} = W_{\{i\}}$ follows from Remark 2.41 and we have that

$$\mathrm{T}_{\{i\}}(V_{\{i\}}) = \mathrm{T}_{\{i\}}(W_{\{i\}}) = \{0_n\} \quad \text{or} \quad \mathrm{T}_{\{i\}}(V_{\{i\}}) = \mathrm{T}_{\{i\}}(W_{\{i\}}) = \mathbb{F}_2^n .$$

In either case, the condition that S'_i maps $\mathcal{L}(\mathrm{T}_{\{i\}}(V_{\{i\}}))$ to $\mathcal{L}(\mathrm{T}_{\{i\}}(W_{\{i\}}))$ is trivial, and any S-box fulfills it. As a consequence, an independent inactive S-box can be freely chosen. In other words, such an S-box has no impact on the fact that σ maps $\mathcal{L}(V)$ to $\mathcal{L}(W)$.

Finally, suppose that some S-boxes are linked together. If only one of these S-boxes is replaced independently of the others, then the desired property of the substitution layer may not hold.

Example 2.42. As we have seen in Example 2.38 and **Figure 2.11**, the least decomposition partition with regard to the subspaces V and W is $\mathcal{I}_{\mathrm{ld}} = \{\{1\}, \{2\}, \{0, 3\}\}$. By Proposition 2.33, the substitution layer maps $\mathcal{L}(V)$ to $\mathcal{L}(W)$ is and only if the following equalities hold:

$$\sigma_{\{0,3\}}(\mathcal{L}(\mathrm{T}_{\{0,3\}}(V))) = \mathcal{L}(\mathrm{T}_{\{0,3\}}(W)), \qquad \begin{aligned} S_1(\mathcal{L}(\mathrm{T}_{\{1\}}(V)) &= \mathcal{L}(\mathrm{T}_{\{1\}}(W)), \\ S_2(\mathcal{L}(\mathrm{T}_{\{2\}}(V)) &= \mathcal{L}(\mathrm{T}_{\{2\}}(W)). \end{aligned}$$

Thus, the S-box S_1 is independent of the other S-boxes, the same applies to S_2 and the S-boxes S_0 and S_3 are linked together. As was already noted in **Figure 2.9**, we have that

$$V_{\{1\}} = \{(\texttt{00}, \texttt{00}, \texttt{00}, \texttt{00})\} \quad \text{and} \quad V_{\{2\}} = \mathrm{span}((\texttt{00}, \texttt{00}, \texttt{1A}, \texttt{00}), (\texttt{00}, \texttt{00}, \texttt{07}, \texttt{00})) .$$

Therefore, the S-box S_2 is active while S_1 is inactive. ▲

3.4. The forbidden case

Throughout this section, we assume that the substitution layer σ maps $\mathcal{L}(V)$ to $\mathcal{L}(W)$. In order to prove the last main theorem of this chapter, we need to consider the following particular case.

Proposition 2.43. Let $\mathcal{I}$ be a decomposition partition. Let I be a part of $\mathcal{I}$ such that $\#I \geq 2$ and let E be a nonempty proper subset of I. Suppose that $V_E = V_{I\setminus E} = \{0_{nm}\}$ and $\mathrm{P}_E(V) = \mathrm{Triv}_E$. Then, for all i in E, S_i is an affine mapping.

If the subspace V satisfies the assumption of the proposition above, then at least one of S-boxes has to be affine. Nowadays, an SPN whose substitution layer has an affine S-box cannot be taken seriously. Additionally, such a cipher is likely to be very weak to differential and linear cryptanalysis. This discussion explains the title of this section.

Example 2.44. As seen in Example 2.38, the least decomposition partition is $\mathcal{I}_{\text{ld}} = \{\{1\}, \{2\}, \{0, 3\}\}$. Its only part of cardinality greater than or equal to 2 is $I = \{0, 3\}$. The nonempty proper subsets of I are the $E = \{0\}$ and $E = \{1\}$. According to **Figure 2.9**, we have $V_{\{0\}} \neq \{0_{20}\}$. Consequently, Proposition 2.43 does not apply to this example, and this is good news because none of the S-boxes is affine. Otherwise, this would have disproved the contrapositive of Proposition 2.43.

Now let us introduce another example. Consider a substitution layer σ' made up of two 3-bit S-boxes S'_0 and S'_1; hence, its parameters are $m = 2$ and $n = 3$. Define the subspaces V' and W' of $(\mathbb{F}_2^3)^2$ by

$$V' = W' = \text{span}((4, 4), (2, 2), (1, 1)) = \{(x, x) | x \in \mathbb{F}_2^3\}.$$

Finally, suppose that σ' maps $\mathcal{L}(V')$ to $\mathcal{L}(W')$. It is easily seen that

$$V'_{\varnothing} = \{(0, 0)\}, \quad V'_{\{0\}} = \{(0, 0)\}, \quad V'_{\{1\}} = \{(0, 0)\}, \quad V'_{\{0,1\}} = V,$$

$$\mathrm{P}_{\varnothing}(V') = \mathrm{Triv}_{\varnothing}, \quad \mathrm{P}_{\{0\}}(V') = \mathrm{Triv}_{\{0\}}, \quad \mathrm{P}_{\{1\}}(V') = \mathrm{Triv}_{\{1\}}, \quad \mathrm{P}_{\{0,1\}}(V') = V.$$

Thus, the least decomposition partition with regard to V' and W' is $\{\{0, 1\}\}$. The S-boxes S'_0 and S'_1 are then linked together. Choosing $E = \{0\}$ in Proposition 2.43 ensures that S'_0 must be affine. Similarly, we can prove that S'_1 must also be affine by considering $E = \{1\}$. As a result, any substitution layer σ' mapping $\mathcal{L}(V')$ to $\mathcal{L}(W')$ is necessary affine. These subspaces are thus completely prohibited as the whole cipher is then affine. ▲

3.5. Reduction to one S-box

To prove our main result about the substitution layer, we need the following preliminary lemma.

Lemma 2.45. Let I be a part of $\mathcal{I}_{\text{ld}}$ and E be a non-empty proper subset of I.

- If V_E is a trivial product subspace, then $V_E = \mathrm{Triv}_{\varnothing} = \{0_{nm}\}$.
- If $\mathrm{P}_E(V)$ is a trivial product subspace, then $\mathrm{P}_E(V) = \mathrm{Triv}_E$.

Now we have all the results needed, let us state and prove the main result of Section 3 which is depicted in **Figure 2.12.**

Theorem 2.46. Let $n \geq 2$ and m be two positive integers. Let $S_0, \ldots, S_{m-1}$ be n-bit S-boxes. Define the permutation σ of $(\mathbb{F}_2^n)^m$, which maps the element $(x_i)_{0 \leq i < m}$ to $(S_i(x_i))_{0 \leq i < m}$. Let V and W be two subspaces of $(\mathbb{F}_2^n)^m$ such that σ maps $\mathcal{L}(V)$ to $\mathcal{L}(W)$. Suppose that V is not a trivial product subspace. Then, at least one of the S-boxes maps a nontrivial linear partition to another one.

http://dx.doi.org/10.5772/intechopen.70420

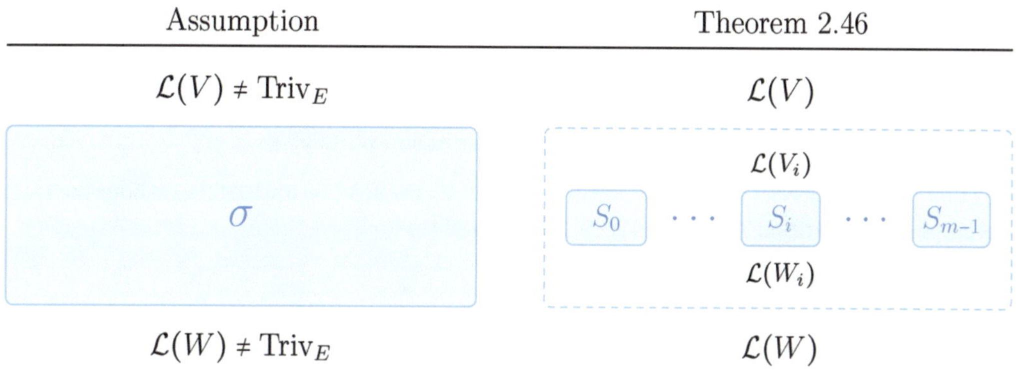

Figure 2.12. Diagrammatic representation of Theorem 2.46.

Proof. Let us prove this result by complete induction on the number m of S-boxes. Suppose that $m = 1$. In this case, $\sigma = S_0$. By hypothesis, V is different from $\{0_n\}$ and $\mathbb{F}_2^n$. Hence, $\mathcal{L}(V)$ is a nontrivial partition and S_0 maps $\mathcal{L}(V)$ to $\mathcal{L}(W)$.

Let $m \geq 2$ be an integer. Suppose that the result holds for any positive integer strictly lower than m. First, suppose that all the S-boxes are independent. In other words, $\mathcal{I}_{\mathrm{ld}} = \{\{i\} | i \in [\![0,m[\![\}$. If each S-box is inactive, then V is a trivial product subspace, a contradiction with our hypothesis. Thus, there exists at least one active S-box S_i. In this case, $\{0_{nm}\} \not\subseteq V_{\{i\}} \not\subseteq \mathrm{Triv}_{\{i\}}$. According to Lemma 2.31, the equality $\mathrm{P}_{\{i\}}(V) = V_{\{i\}}$ holds. Then, $\mathrm{T}_{\{i\}}(V_{\{i\}}) = \mathrm{T}_{\{i\}}(\mathrm{P}_{\{i\}}(V)) = \mathrm{T}_{\{i\}}(V)$ is a nontrivial subspace of $\mathbb{F}_2^n$, so $\mathcal{L}(\mathrm{T}_{\{i\}}(V))$ is also nontrivial. Finally, Proposition 2.22 states that S_i maps $\mathcal{L}(\mathrm{T}_{\{i\}}(V))$ to $\mathcal{L}(\mathrm{T}_{\{i\}}(W))$, and thus the result holds in this case.

Now, suppose that some S-boxes are linked together. Then, there exists an element I of $\mathcal{I}_{\mathrm{ld}}$ such that $I \geq 2$. Next, at least one of the following three cases holds.

1. Suppose that there exists a nonempty proper subset E of I such that $\mathrm{P}_E(V)$ is not a trivial product subspace. Let p denote the cardinality of E. Recall that $\mathrm{T}_E(\mathrm{P}_E(V)) = \mathrm{T}_E(V)$. It follows that $\mathrm{T}_E(V)$ is not a trivial product subspace of $(\mathbb{F}_2^n)^p$. According to Proposition 2.22, σ_E maps $\mathcal{L}(\mathrm{T}_E(V))$ to $\mathcal{L}(\mathrm{T}_E(W))$. Note that E is a non-empty proper subset of I, so of $[\![0,m[\![$. Hence $p < m$, so the induction hypothesis ensures that at least one of the S-boxes of σ_m maps a nontrivial partition to another one.

2. Suppose that there exists a nonempty proper subset E of I such that V_E is not a trivial product subspace. Recall that σ maps $\mathcal{L}(V_E)$ to $\mathcal{L}(W_E)$. Proposition 2.22 ensures that σ_E maps $\mathcal{L}(\mathrm{T}_E(V_E))$ to $\mathcal{L}(\mathrm{T}_E(W_E))$. It is easily seen that $\mathrm{T}_E(V_E)$ is not a trivial product subspace. As before, the result is a consequence of the induction hypothesis.

3. Suppose that there exists a nonempty proper subset E of I such that $\mathrm{P}_E(V)$, V_E and $V_{I \setminus E}$ are all trivial product subspaces. Then, Lemma 2.45 implies that $\mathrm{P}_E(V) = \mathrm{Triv}_E$ and $V_E = V_{I \setminus E} = \{0_{nm}\}$. According to Proposition 2.43, the S-boxes whose indices belong to E are affine mappings. Combining Proposition 2.15 and 2.13, we see that these S-boxes map any non-trivial linear partition to another one.

In any case, the result holds for this integer m. The result follows by induction. ▪

Example 2.47. It is worthwhile to note that the proof of Theorem 2.46 is constructive. Therefore, it gives a method to find necessary conditions on the S-boxes for the substitution layer to map $\mathcal{L}(V)$ to $\mathcal{L}(W)$. Let us apply this method to our main example.

The first step is equivalent to what had been done in Examples 2.38 and 2.42. Consider the least decomposition partition $\mathcal{I}_{\mathrm{ld}} = \{\{1\}, \{2\}, \{0,3\}\}$ and deduce that:

- S_1 is inactive;
- S_2 is active and maps $\mathcal{L}(\mathrm{span}(\mathtt{07}, \mathtt{1A}))$ to $\mathcal{L}(\mathrm{span}(\mathtt{0E}, \mathtt{12}))$ (see **Figure 2.2**);
- S_0 and S_3 are linked together.

Now, consider the part $I = \{0,3\}$ of $\mathcal{I}_{\mathrm{ld}}$. Thus, the nonempty proper subsets of I are $\{0\}$ and $\{3\}$. The first case requires to compute the following projections:

$$\mathrm{P}_{\{0\}}(V) = \mathrm{Triv}_{\{0\}} \quad \text{and} \quad \mathrm{P}_{\{3\}}(V) = \mathrm{span}((\mathtt{00}, \mathtt{00}, \mathtt{00}, \mathtt{0B}), (\mathtt{00}, \mathtt{00}, \mathtt{00}, \mathtt{1C}))\,.$$

Thus, $\mathrm{P}_{\{3\}}(V)$ is not a trivial product subspace. As in Example 2.24 and **Figure 2.8**, we see that S_3 maps $\mathcal{L}(\mathtt{0B}, \mathtt{1C})$ to $\mathcal{L}(\mathtt{08}, \mathtt{15})$ by truncating σ and the subspaces $\mathrm{P}_{\{3\}}(V)$, $\mathrm{P}_{\{3\}}(W)$ to $\{3\}$. Now, we need to compute the following subspaces:

$$V_{\{0\}} = \mathrm{span}((\mathtt{03}, \mathtt{00}, \mathtt{00}, \mathtt{00}), (\mathtt{0D}, \mathtt{00}, \mathtt{00}, \mathtt{00}), (\mathtt{15}, \mathtt{00}, \mathtt{00}, \mathtt{00})) \quad \text{and} \quad V_{\{3\}} = \mathrm{Triv}_{\varnothing}\,.$$

Since $V_{\{0\}}$ is not a trivial product subspace, the second case apply. Then, truncate the substitution layer σ and the subspaces $V_{\{0\}}$ and $W_{\{0\}}$ to prove that S_0 maps $\mathcal{L}(\mathtt{03}, \mathtt{0D}, \mathtt{15})$ to $\mathcal{L}(\mathtt{01}, \mathtt{0E}, \mathtt{14})$. This property was stressed in Example 2.28 and **Figure 2.9.** Finally, recall that the third case does not apply to these subspaces, as observed in Example 2.44. ▲

The preceding example covers only the first and the second cases in the treatment of linked S-boxes given by the proof of Theorem 2.46. To illustrate the third case, we introduced the following example.

Example 2.48. Let $n = m = 3$. Thus, the substitution layer σ is made up of three 3-bit S-boxes denoted by S_0, S_1 and S_2. Define the subspaces V and W of $(\mathbb{F}_2^3)^3$ by

$$V = W = \{(x, y, x + y) \mid x, y \in \mathbb{F}_2^3\}$$

and assume that the substitution layer σ maps $\mathcal{L}(V)$ to $\mathcal{L}(W)$. By definition, it holds that $\mathrm{P}_{\varnothing}(V) = \{(0, 0, 0)\}$ and $\mathrm{P}_{\{0,1,2\}}(V) = V$. Then, for each nonempty proper subset E of $\{0,1,2\}$, it is easily seen that $\mathrm{P}_E(V) = \mathrm{Triv}_E$. For instance,

$$\mathrm{P}_{\{0,1\}}(V) = \{(x, y, 0) | x, y \in \mathbb{F}_2^3\} = \mathrm{Triv}_{\{0,1\}}\,.$$

We know that $V_{\varnothing} = \{(0, 0, 0)\}$ and $V_{\{0,1,2\}}(V) = V$. The other subspaces V_E are the following:

$$V_{\{0\}} = \{(0,0,0)\}, \qquad V_{\{1\}} = \{(0,0,0)\}, \qquad V_{\{2\}} = \{(0,0,0)\},$$
$$V_{\{0,1\}} = \{(x,x,0) | x \in \mathbb{F}_2^3\}, \quad V_{\{0,2\}} = \{(x,0,x) | x \in \mathbb{F}_2^3\}, \quad V_{\{1,2\}} = \{(0,x,x) | x \in \mathbb{F}_2^3\}.$$

Thus, the equality $P_E(V) = V_E$ holds only for $E = \varnothing$ and $E = \{0,1,2\}$. Consequently, the least decomposition partition is $\mathcal{I}_{\mathrm{ld}} = \{\{0, 1, 2\}\}$, and hence, all the S-boxes are linked together.

From now on, we follow the method given in the proof of Theorem 2.46. As previously noted, for each nonempty proper subset E of {0,1,2}, the projection $P_E(V)$ is a trivial product. Therefore, the first case does not apply to this example. We move on to the second case. By induction, the substitution layer and the subspaces $V_{\{0,1\}}$ and $W_{\{0,1\}}$ are truncated to {0,1}. Hence, we now consider the permutation $\sigma' = \sigma_{\{0,1\}}$, which maps $\mathcal{L}(V')$ to $\mathcal{L}(W')$ where

$$V' = W' = \mathrm{T}_{\{0,1\}}(V_{\{0,1\}}) = \{(x,x) | x \in \mathbb{F}_2^3\}.$$

Such a substitution layer has already been studied in Example 2.44. Recall that

$$V'_{\varnothing} = \{(0,0)\}, \quad V'_{\{0\}} = \{(0,0)\}, \quad V'_{\{1\}} = \{(0,0)\}, \quad V'_{\{0,1\}} = V,$$
$$P_{\varnothing}(V') = \mathrm{Triv}_{\varnothing}, \quad P_{\{0\}}(V') = \mathrm{Triv}_{\{0\}}, \quad P_{\{1\}}(V') = \mathrm{Triv}_{\{1\}}, \quad P_{\{0,1\}}(V') = V.$$

Thus, the least decomposition partition with regard to V' and W' is {{0,1}}. Since $V'_{\{0\}}$, $V'_{\{1\}}$, $P_{\{0\}}(V')$ and $P_{\{1\}}(V')$ are all trivial products, the first and second cases do not apply. Choosing $E = \{0\}$ and $E = \{1\}$ in the third case proves that S_0 and S_1 are affine mappings. Come back to the full substitution layer. Similarly, it is straightforward to verify that S_2 must be affine by truncating σ and the subspaces $V_{\{0,2\}}$, $W_{\{0,2\}}$ to {0,2}. To summarize, we have proven that any substitution layer mapping $\mathcal{L}(V)$ to $\mathcal{L}(W)$ is necessarily affine. ▲

In this chapter, we have studied a generic SPN mapping a partition $\mathcal{A}$ of $\mathbb{F}_2^{nm}$ to a partition $\mathcal{B}$ of $\mathbb{F}_2^{nm}$, independently of the round keys used. Combining Theorem 2.17 and Corollary 2.18, we proved that there exist two families $(V^{[i]})_{0 \le i \le r}$ and $(W^{[i]})_{0 \le i \le r}$ of subspaces of $\mathbb{F}_2^{nm}$ such that the substitution layer σ maps $\mathcal{L}(V^{[i]})$ to $\mathcal{L}(W^{[i]})$ for each $0 \le i \le r$. This result has been illustrated in **Figure 2.5.**

First, suppose that all the $V^{[i]}$ are trivial products. In such a case, the diffusion layer of the cipher is probably not playing its role (or the round number is very small). As is generally the case, suppose that there is no diffusion layer in the last round of the SPN. Then, the input and the output partitions are both linear partitions associated with a trivial product subspace. This implies that some ciphertext bits are independent of some plaintext bits. Such a property must be avoided in any good cipher.

Now, suppose that at least one of the $V^{[i]}$ is not a trivial product. This second case is far more interesting than the previous one. By virtue of Theorem 2.46, at least one of the S-boxes must map a nontrivial linear partition to another one, as illustrated in **Figure 2.12.**

Thus, we have proven in this chapter that any good partition-based trapdoor SPN has at least on S-box mapping a nontrivial linear partition to another one. The following chapter aims to design such an S-box with the best security against both differential and linear cryptanalysis.

Analysis of a backdoor S-box

Differential [21] and linear [22] cryptanalysis are considered as the most important attacks against block ciphers [23]. The resistance of an S-box against these attacks is assessed by its difference distribution table and its linear approximation table respectively.

Let S be an n-bit S-box. The difference distribution table and the linear distribution table of S are the two families DT_S and LT_S indexed by $(\mathbb{F}_2^n)^2$ and defined for any (a, b) in $(\mathbb{F}_2^n)^2$ by

$$DT_S(a,b) = \#\{x \in \mathbb{F}_2^n \mid S(x) + S(x+a) = b\},$$

$$LT_S(a,b) = \#\{x \in \mathbb{F}_2^n \mid \langle a,x\rangle = \langle b, S(x)\rangle\} - 2^{n-1}.$$

Moreover, the S-box S is said to be *differentially δ-uniform* if $\mathrm{DT}_S(a,b) \leq \delta$ for any (a, b) in $(\mathbb{F}_2^n)^2$ with $a \neq 0$. Similarly, S is *linearly λ-uniform* if $|\mathrm{LT}_S(a,b)| \leq \lambda$ for every (a, b) in $(\mathbb{F}_2^n)^2$ with $b \neq 0$. It is worthwhile to mention that the smaller the differential uniformity is, the more resistant S is against differential cryptanalysis. The same applies for linear cryptanalysis.

Remark 3.1. It can be proven that any n-bit S-box is at least linearly $2^{\frac{n-1}{2}}$-uniform.

Recall that two permutations S_1 and S_2 of $\mathbb{F}_2^n$ are said to be *equivalent* if there exist two linear mappings L_1, L_2 of $\mathbb{F}_2^n$ and two elements v_1, v_2 of $\mathbb{F}_2^n$ such that

$$\forall x \in \mathbb{F}_2^n, \quad S_2(x) = L_2(S_1(L_1(x) + v_1)) + v_2.$$

It is well known that equivalent permutations have the same differential uniformity and the same linear uniformity, see for instance [24, 25]. More precisely, their differential tables are equal up to row and column permutations. This result holds for linear tables up to the sign of the coefficients.

Let V and W be two subspaces of $\mathbb{F}_2^n$. Suppose that S' is an n-bit S-Box mapping $\mathcal{L}(V)$ to $\mathcal{L}(W)$. Proposition 2.11 ensures that there exists an automorphism L of $\mathbb{F}_2^n$ such that $L(V) = W$. Since $L^{-1}(W) = V$, Proposition 2.15 states that L^{-1} maps $\mathcal{L}(W)$ to $\mathcal{L}(V)$. Then, $S = L^{-1} \circ S'$ is equivalent to S' and maps $\mathcal{L}(V)$ to $\mathcal{L}(V)$. This discussion establishes the following proposition.

Proposition 3.2. Let V and W be two subspaces of $\mathbb{F}_2^n$. If S' is an n-bit S-box mapping $\mathcal{L}(V)$ to $\mathcal{L}(W)$, then there exists an S-box S equivalent to S' preserving $\mathcal{L}(V)$.

Remark 3.3. Conversely, suppose that S preserves $\mathcal{L}(V)$. Let W be any subspace isomorphic to V. Then find an automorphism L such that $L(V) = W$. By Proposition 2.15, $L \circ S$ maps $\mathcal{L}(V)$ to $\mathcal{L}(W)$.

As with Section 3, let us introduce an example that we will continue throughout this section.

Example 3.4. Consider the 5-bit S-box S' given in **Figure 3.1.** This S-box has already been met twice in Examples 2.7 and 2.19 (refered to as f and S_2 respectively). Thus, we know that S'

http://dx.doi.org/10.5772/intechopen.70420

		.0	.1	.2	.3	.4	.5	.6	.7	.8	.9	.A	.B	.C	.D	.E	.F
$S'(x)$	0.	1E	08	04	13	0F	18	14	10	19	15	0E	0D	03	1C	07	17
	1.	12	11	0B	1B	09	05	1F	00	0A	01	02	1A	06	0C	1D	16
$L^{-1}(x)$	0.	00	01	02	03	08	09	0A	0B	0D	0C	0F	0E	05	04	07	06
	1.	18	19	1A	1B	10	11	12	13	15	14	17	16	1D	1C	1F	1E
$S(x)$	0.	1F	0D	08	1B	06	15	10	18	14	11	07	04	03	1D	0B	13
	1.	1A	19	0E	16	0C	09	1E	00	0F	01	02	17	0A	05	1C	12

Figure 3.1. Construction of the S-box S used throughout Chapter 3.

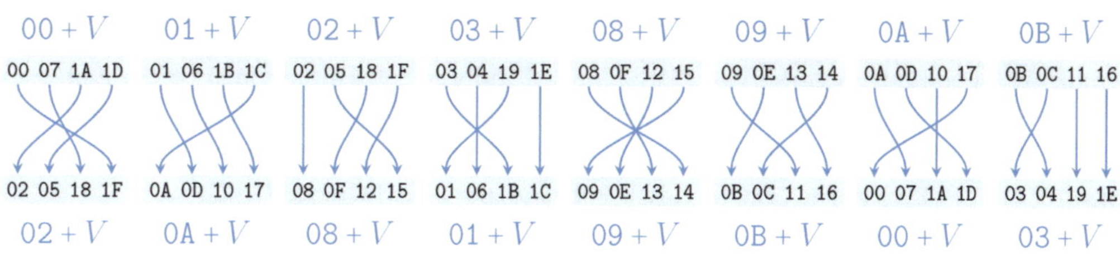

Figure 3.2. The permutation S preserving $\mathcal{L}(V)$ where $V = \text{span}(\texttt{07}, \texttt{1A})$.

maps $\mathcal{L}(V)$ to $\mathcal{L}(W)$ where $V = \text{span}(\texttt{07}, \texttt{1A})$ and $W = \text{span}(\texttt{0E}, \texttt{12})$. Following the proof of Proposition 2.11, an automorphism L of $\mathbb{F}_2^5$ satisfying $L(V) = W$ was constructed in Example 2.12. Its inverse L^{-1} and the composition $S = L^{-1}S'$ are given in **Figure 3.1.** For instance, $S(\texttt{07}) = L^{-1}(S'(\texttt{07})) = L^{-1}(\texttt{10}) = \texttt{18}$. It is easy to check in **Figure 3.2** that S preserves the linear partition $\mathcal{L}(V)$. Finally, it is worth observing how **Figures 2.2** and **3.2** look similar. This explains our choices to construct the automorphism L. ▲

By virtue of Proposition 3.2, we can assume without loss of generality that $V = W$ in our study of the linear and differential properties of an S-box mapping $\mathcal{L}(V)$ to $\mathcal{L}(W)$.

Throughout this section, we consider the following

- let V be a d-dimensional nontrivial subspace of $\mathbb{F}_2^n$,
- let U be a complement space of V,
- let S be an n-bit S-box preserving $\mathcal{L}(V)$.

Therefore, the space $\mathbb{F}_2^n$ can be written as the direct sum $U \oplus V$. In other words, every element x of $\mathbb{F}_2^n$ can be uniquely written as the sum $x = u + v$ where u and v belong to U and V, respectively. Let $[u]$ denote the coset of V with respect to u. Thus, $[u] = u + V$ is the unique part of $\mathcal{L}(V)$ where u lies in and we have

$$\mathcal{L}(V) = \{[u] | u \in U\}.$$

Since V is d-dimensional, the complement space U is $(n - d)$-dimensional. In addition, we have the following inequalities

$$1 \le d \le n - 1 \quad \text{and} \quad 1 \le n - d \le n - 1$$

because V is assumed to be a nontrivial subspace of $\mathbb{F}_2^n$.

The following theorem describes the structure of permutations preserving a linear partition. It can be seen as a corollary of the Krasner-Kaloujnine embedding theorem [26]. However, for convenience, we give a direct constructive proof.

Theorem 3.5. There exist a unique permutation ρ of U and a unique family of permutations $(\tau_u)_{u\in U}$ of V such that, for all $x = u + v$ in $\mathbb{F}_2^n$,

$$S(u+v) = \rho(u) + \tau_u(v) \; .$$

Conversely, if ρ is a permutation of U and if $(\tau_u)_{u\in U}$ is a family of permutations of V, then the mapping S' defined by $S'(u+v) = \rho(u) + \tau_u(v)$ preserves $\mathcal{L}(V)$.

Proof. By hypothesis, S preserves $\mathcal{L}(V)$. Thus, S induces a permutation ρ of U defined as follows. Let u be an element of U. Hence, there exists a unique u' in U such as $f([u]) = [u']$. Define then $\rho(u) = u'$. For each element u of U, define the permutation τ_u of V, which maps v to $S(u+v) + \rho(u)$. By construction, for any u in U and any v in V, we have

$$\tau_u(v) = S(u+v) + \rho(u) \quad \text{and hence} \quad S(u+v) = \rho(u) + \tau_u(v).$$

The existence of the permutations ρ and τ_u is proven. Now, let us show their uniqueness. Suppose that there exist a permutation $\tilde{\rho}$ of U and a family of permutations $(\tilde{\tau}_u)_{u\in U}$ of V satisfying the result. Let (u, v) be an element of $U \times V$. By hypothesis, we have

$$\rho(u) + \tau_u(v) = \tilde{\rho}(u) + \tilde{\tau}_u(v) \; .$$

Because the sum of U and V is direct, it follows that $\rho(u) = \tilde{\rho}(u)$ and $\tau_u(v) = \tilde{\tau}_u(v)$. The uniqueness of ρ and the τ_u follows.

Conversely, let ρ be a permutation of U and $(\tau_u)_{u\in U}$ be a family of permutations of V. Denote S' the mapping from $\mathbb{F}_2^n$ to $\mathbb{F}_2^n$ defined by $S'(u+v) = \rho(u) + \tau_u(v)$. Since $\mathbb{F}_2^n = U \oplus V$ and ρ and the τ_u are permutations of U and V respectively, The mapping S' is a permutation of $\mathbb{F}_2^n$. Let u be an element of U. It holds that

$$\begin{aligned} S'([u]) &= \{S'(u+v) | v \in V\} = \{\rho(u) + \tau_u(v) | v \in V\} \\ &= \rho(u) + \{\tau_u(v) | v \in V\} = \rho(u) + V = [\rho(u)] \; . \end{aligned}$$

Hence, S' preserves the linear partition $\mathcal{L}(V)$. ∎

This theorem allows us to design an S-box that preserves $\mathcal{L}(V)$ using permutations with smaller domains. Furthermore, these permutations can be chosen arbitrarily.

Example 3.6. Consider the complement subspace U of V defined by

$$U = \text{span}(\texttt{01}, \texttt{02}, \texttt{08}) = \{\texttt{00}, \texttt{01}, \texttt{02}, \texttt{03}, \texttt{08}, \texttt{09}, \texttt{0A}, \texttt{0B}\} \; .$$

Figure 3.2 shows that S induces a permutation ρ of U. For instance, $\rho(00) = 02$ because S maps the part [00] to [02]. The whole permutation ρ is given in **Figure 3.3.** For each u in U, define the permutation τ_u of V by $\tau_u(v) = S(u+v) + \rho(u)$. For example,

$$\tau_{02}(\texttt{1D}) = S(\texttt{02} + \texttt{1D}) + \rho(\texttt{02}) = S(\texttt{1F}) + \rho(\texttt{02}) = \texttt{12} + \texttt{08} = \texttt{1A}.$$

The permutations τ_u are also given in **Figure 3.3.** Informally, the permutation ρ tells us how S permutes the parts of $\mathcal{L}(V)$ and the permutations $(\tau_u)_{u\in U}$ describe how the elements are moved inside each part (**Figure 3.4**). ▲

In the rest of this section, the permutation ρ and the family $(\tau_u)_{u\in U}$ given by Theorem 3.5 are fixed.

The goal of this part is to express the linear and differential properties of S according to the ones of the permutations ρ and $(\tau_u)_{u\in U}$. However, these permutations are not defined on $\mathbb{F}_2^n$ but on the subspaces U and V of $\mathbb{F}_2^n$. Thus, the concept of linear or differential table is inexistent for such maps. To solve this problem, we define two isomorphisms between U and $\mathbb{F}_2^{n-d}$ and between V and $\mathbb{F}_2^d$. Then, we consider the maps induced by ρ and $(\tau_u)_{u\in U}$ on these spaces.

Notation 3.7. Let $\mathcal{B}_U = (u_i)_{i<n-d}$ and $\mathcal{B}_V = (v_i)_{i<n-d}$ be two bases of U and V respectively. Define the following mappings:

$$\begin{aligned} L_U : \mathbb{F}_2^{n-d} &\to U & \qquad L_V : \mathbb{F}_2^{d} &\to V \\ (x_{n-d-1},\dots,x_0) &\mapsto \sum_{i-0}^{n-d-1} x_i u_i, & (y_{d-1},\dots,y_0) &\mapsto \sum_{i=0}^{d-1} y_i v_i. \end{aligned}$$

It is easily seen that L_U and L_V are both isomorphisms of vector spaces. Define the permutation $\rho' = L_U^{-1}\rho L_U$ of $\mathbb{F}_2^{n-d}$. Finally, for each u in U, let τ'_u denote the permutation $L_V^{-1}\tau_u L_V$ of $\mathbb{F}_2^d$.

Example 3.8. Consider the bases $\mathcal{B}_U = (\texttt{01}, \texttt{02}, \texttt{08})$ and $\mathcal{B}_V = (\texttt{07}, \texttt{1A})$ and define the isomorphisms L_U and L_V. The permutation ρ' of $\mathbb{F}_2^3$ and the permutations τ'_u of $\mathbb{F}_2^2$ are given in **Figure 3.5.** ▲

1. Linear approximation table

The next theorem links the linear tables of S and ρ'. The coefficients of the linear approximation table of S taken into account by this result are in practice the greatest. Thus, they generally determine the linear uniformity of S.

Theorem 3.9. Let a and b be two elements of $V^\perp$. Denote $a^t = L_U^\intercal(a)$ and $b^t = L_U^\intercal(b)$. Then,

$$LT_S(a,b) = 2^d \times LT_{\rho'}(a^t, b^t)\,.$$

Remark 3.10. Consider the map $L_U^\intercal : \mathbb{F}_2^n \to \mathbb{F}_2^{n-d}$. Then, $\ker(L_U^\intercal) = (\mathrm{Im} L_U)^\perp = U^\perp$. Observe that $U^\perp \cap V^\perp = (U+V)^\perp = (\mathbb{F}_2^n)^\perp = \{0\}$. Consequently, the restriction $L_U^\intercal : V^\perp \to \mathbb{F}_2^{n-d}$ is one-to-one and thus onto because of the rank-nullity theorem.

Example 3.11. The restriction $L_U^\intercal : V^\perp \to \mathbb{F}_2^3$ is given by the following table.

a	00	05	0B	0E	13	16	18	1D
$L_U^\intercal(a)$	0	1	7	6	3	2	4	5

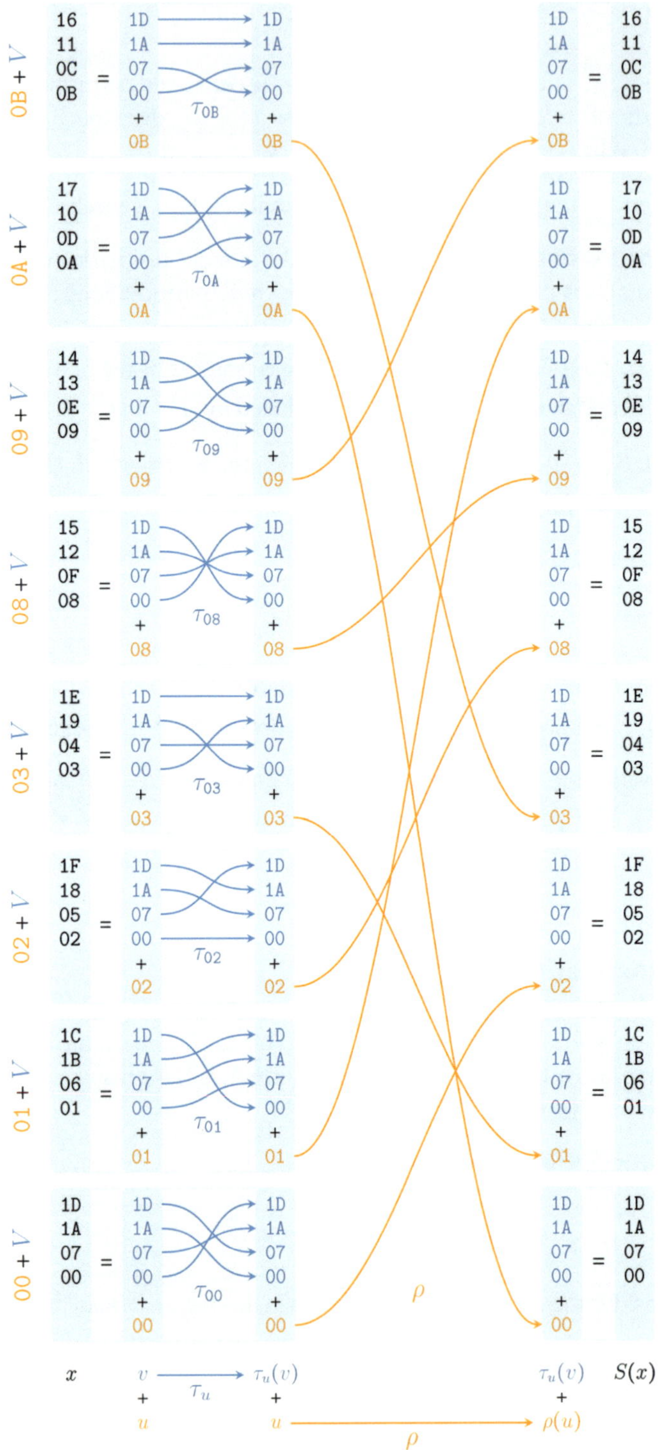

Figure 3.3. The permutation S preserving $\mathcal{L}(V)$ where $V = \text{span}(\texttt{07}, \texttt{1A})$.

x	0	1	2	3	4	5	6	7
$L_U(x)$	00	01	02	03	08	09	0A	0B

x	0	1	2	3
$L_V(x)$	00	07	1A	1D

Figure 3.4. The linear transformations L_U and L_V.

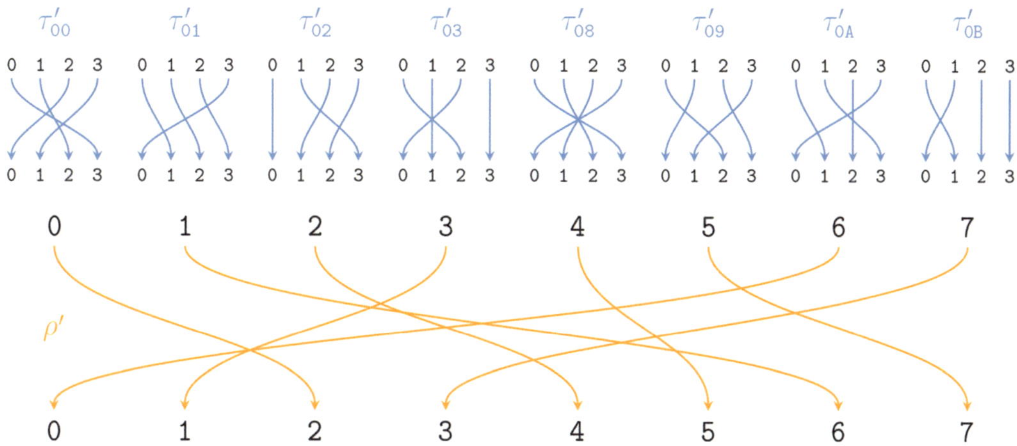

Figure 3.5. The family of permutations $(\tau'_u)_{u \in U}$ and the permutation ρ'.

Reorder the rows and the columns of the linear approximation table of S to begin with $((L_U^\mathsf{T})^{-1}(x))_{x \in \mathbb{F}_2^3}$, as suggested by Theorem 3.9. The reordered linear table is shown in **Figure 3.6.** Each dot "·" in this figure stands for the integer 0. With this order, it is easily seen that the top left part of LT_S is exactly the linear table of ρ' multiplied by $2^d = 4$. For instance, $\mathrm{LT}_S(\mathtt{1D}, \mathtt{16}) = 2^2 \times \mathrm{LT}_{\rho'}(5, 2) = -8$ because $L_U^\mathsf{T}(\mathtt{1D}) = 5$ and $L_U^\mathsf{T}(\mathtt{16}) = 2$. ▲

Corollary 3.12. The S-box S is at least linearly $2^{(n+d-1)/2}$-uniform.

Proof. As noted in Remark 3.1, there exist two elements a^t and b^t of $\mathbb{F}_2^{n-d}$ both nonzero such that $|\mathrm{LT}_{\rho'}(a^t, b^t)| \geq 2^{(n-d-1)/2}$. Let a and b denote the elements $(L_U^\mathsf{T})^{-1}(a^t)$ and $(L_U^\mathsf{T})^{-1}(b^t)$ of $\mathbb{F}_2^n$. Then, Theorem 3.9 implies that

$$|\mathrm{LT}_S(a, b)| = 2^d \times |\mathrm{LT}_{\rho'}(a^t, b^t)| \geq 2^d \times 2^{(n-d-1)/2} = 2^{(n+d-1)/2}.$$

Observe that a and b are nonzero and the result is proven. ▪

Remark 3.13. It is well-known that any 4-bit S-box is at least linearly 4-uniform, see for example [27]. As a consequence, the permutation S is at least 2^{d+2}-uniform if $n–d = 4$. Similarly, any 2-bit S-Box is linearly 2-uniform, and hence S is at least 2^{d+1}-uniform if $n - d = 2$.

Example 3.14. It is easily seen that S is linearly 8-uniform in **Figure 3.6.** The lower bound given by Corollary 3.12 is $2^{(n+d-1)/2} = 2^{(5+2-1)/2} = 8$. Therefore, this bound is tight on this example. ▲

ρ'

	0	1	2	3	4	5	6	7
0	4	.	.	.	.	.	.	.
1	.	2	2	.	.	2	-2	.
2	.	.	-2	-2	-2	2	.	.
3	.	-2	.	-2	2	.	-2	.
4	.	2	.	-2	.	-2	.	-2
5	.	.	-2	2	.	.	-2	-2
6	.	2	-2	.	2	.	.	2
7	.	.	.	.	2	2	2	-2

	$V^{\top}$																															
	00	05	16	13	18	1D	0E	0B	01	02	03	04	06	07	08	09	0A	0C	0D	0F	10	11	12	14	15	17	19	1A	1B	1C	1E	1F
$V^{\top}$ 00	16	·	·	·	·	·	·	·	·	·	·	·	·	·	·	·	·	·	·	·	·	·	·	·	·	·	·	·	·	·	·	·
05	·	8	8	·	·	8	-8	·	·	·	·	·	·	·	·	·	·	·	·	·	·	·	·	·	·	·	·	·	·	·	·	·
16	·	·	-8	-8	-8	8	·	·	·	·	·	·	·	·	·	·	·	·	·	·	·	·	·	·	·	·	·	·	·	·	·	·
13	·	-8	·	-8	8	·	-8	·	·	·	·	·	·	·	·	·	·	·	·	·	·	·	·	·	·	·	·	·	·	·	·	·
18	·	8	·	-8	·	-8	·	-8	·	·	·	·	·	·	·	·	·	·	·	·	·	·	·	·	·	·	·	·	·	·	·	·
1D	·	·	-8	8	·	·	-8	-8	·	·	·	·	·	·	·	·	·	·	·	·	·	·	·	·	·	·	·	·	·	·	·	·
0E	·	8	-8	·	8	·	·	8	·	·	·	·	·	·	·	·	·	·	·	·	·	·	·	·	·	·	·	·	·	·	·	·
0B	·	·	·	·	8	8	8	-8	·	·	·	·	·	·	·	·	·	·	·	·	·	·	·	·	·	·	·	·	·	·	·	·
01	·	·	·	·	·	·	·	·	6	-6	4	-2	·	-2	-4	-2	2	2	·	2	4	-2	-6	2	·	2	-2	-6	-4	-2	·	-2
02	·	·	·	·	·	·	·	·	-6	4	-6	-2	-2	-4	-2	·	2	·	-6	6	2	·	-2	·	-2	2	-2	-4	-2	2	2	4
03	·	·	·	·	·	·	·	·	4	-6	6	·	-2	-2	2	2	·	-2	-6	4	-2	2	4	-2	-2	·	·	2	2	4	2	6
04	·	·	·	·	·	·	·	·	-2	-2	·	-2	4	-6	·	2	2	-2	-4	-6	·	2	2	-2	4	2	-2	-2	·	6	-4	-6
06	·	·	·	·	·	·	·	·	·	2	2	4	2	-2	-2	2	4	6	-2	·	-6	-6	·	-2	2	4	4	2	-2	·	6	-2
07	·	·	·	·	·	·	·	·	-2	·	2	-6	-2	·	-2	4	6	-4	2	2	-6	-4	2	4	-2	-2	2	·	-2	-2	-6	·
08	·	·	·	·	·	·	·	·	4	2	-2	·	6	6	-6	2	·	-2	2	4	-2	2	4	-2	-2	·	·	-6	2	4	2	-2
09	·	·	·	·	·	·	·	·	2	·	-2	-2	2	·	2	-4	2	4	-2	-2	-2	4	6	-4	-6	2	-2	·	-6	-6	-2	·
0A	·	·	·	·	·	·	·	·	-2	-2	·	-2	-4	-6	·	2	-6	-2	4	2	·	2	2	-2	-4	2	6	-2	·	-2	4	-6
0C	·	·	·	·	·	·	·	·	-2	-4	-2	2	-6	4	-6	·	-2	·	-2	2	-2	·	2	·	2	6	-6	4	2	-2	-2	-4
0D	·	·	·	·	·	·	·	·	·	2	2	4	2	-2	-2	-6	4	-2	-2	·	2	2	·	6	-6	4	4	2	6	·	-2	-2
0F	·	·	·	·	·	·	·	·	-2	-6	-4	6	·	-2	4	-2	2	2	·	2	-4	-2	2	2	·	-6	-2	-6	4	-2	·	-2
10	·	·	·	·	·	·	·	·	-4	2	6	·	-2	6	2	2	·	-2	-6	-4	-2	2	-4	-2	-2	·	·	-6	2	-4	2	-2
11	·	·	·	·	·	·	·	·	-2	·	2	2	6	·	6	4	-2	-4	2	2	2	-4	2	4	-2	6	-6	·	-2	-2	2	·
12	·	·	·	·	·	·	·	·	2	-2	-4	-6	·	2	4	2	-2	6	·	-2	-4	2	-2	6	·	6	2	-2	4	2	·	2
14	·	·	·	·	·	·	·	·	2	4	2	-2	-2	-4	-2	·	2	·	2	-2	2	·	6	·	6	2	-2	-4	6	-6	2	4
15	·	·	·	·	·	·	·	·	·	2	2	-4	2	-2	-2	-6	-4	-2	-2	·	-6	2	·	6	2	-4	-4	2	-2	·	6	-2
17	·	·	·	·	·	·	·	·	2	2	·	2	-4	-2	·	6	6	2	4	-2	·	6	-2	2	-4	-2	-6	2	·	2	4	-2
19	·	·	·	·	·	·	·	·	2	2	·	2	4	-2	·	6	-2	2	-4	6	·	6	-2	2	4	-2	2	2	·	-6	-4	-2
1A	·	·	·	·	·	·	·	·	-2	-4	-2	-6	2	4	2	·	6	·	-2	2	6	·	2	·	2	-2	2	4	2	-2	6	-4
1B	·	·	·	·	·	·	·	·	-4	-6	-2	·	6	-2	-6	2	·	-2	2	-4	-2	2	-4	-2	-2	·	·	2	2	-4	2	6
1C	·	·	·	·	·	·	·	·	-6	-2	4	2	·	2	-4	2	-2	6	·	-2	4	2	6	6	·	-2	2	-2	-4	2	·	2
1E	·	·	·	·	·	·	·	·	·	2	2	-4	2	-2	-2	2	-4	6	-2	·	2	-6	·	-2	-6	-4	-4	2	6	·	-2	-2
1F	·	·	·	·	·	·	·	·	-6	·	6	-2	2	·	2	-4	2	4	6	6	-2	4	-2	-4	2	2	-2	·	2	2	-2	·

Figure 3.6. The reordered linear table of *S*.

http://dx.doi.org/10.5772/intechopen.70420

2. Differential distribution table

Unlike linear cryptanalysis, where only a local view of the table was provided, the results for differential cryptanalysis bring both local and global outlooks.

Theorem 3.15. Let $a = u_a + v_a$ and $b = u_b + v_b$ be elements of $\mathbb{F}_2^n$. Denote $u'_a = L_U^{-1}(u_a)$ and $u'_b = L_U^{-1}(u_b)$. Then

$$\sum_{i \in [u_a]} \mathrm{DT}_S(i, b) = \sum_{j \in [u_b]} \mathrm{DT}_S(a, j) = 2^d \times \mathrm{DT}_{\rho'}(u'_a, u'_b)\,.$$

Especially, $\mathrm{DT}_S(a, b) \leq 2^d \times \mathrm{DT}_{\rho'}(u'_a, u'_b)$.

The preceding theorem can be restated in the following way. If DT_S is rearranged coset by coset, a simple operation enables recovery of $\mathrm{DT}\rho'$. On the other hand, the next theorem is similar to Theorem 3.9 but for differential cryptanalysis. Again, it generally highlights the coefficients of DT_S involved in the differential uniformity of S.

Theorem 3.16. Let v_a and v_b be two elements of V. Denote $v'_a = L_V^{-1}(v_a)$ and $v'_b = L_V^{-1}(v_b)$. Then

$$\mathrm{DT}_S(v_a, v_b) = \sum_{u \in U} \mathrm{DT}_{\tau'_u}(v'_a, v'_b)\,.$$

Particularly, the subtable $(\mathrm{DT}_S(v_a, v_b))_{v_a, v_b \in V}$ is uniquely determined by the differential tables $(\mathrm{DT}_{\tau'_u})_{u \in U}$.

Example 3.17. To illustrate Theorems 3.15 and 3.16, reorder the rows and the columns of the differential table of S as presented in **Figure 3.7.** With this order, we can see the differential table of ρ' by considering the differential table of S coset by coset. In fact, Theorem 3.15 states that the sum of all elements in the same row or column of the subtable $\mathrm{DT}_S([u_1], [u_2])$ is equal to the coefficient (x_1, x_2) of $\mathrm{DT}_{\rho'}$ multiplied by 2^2, where $x_i = L_V^{-1}(u_i)$. For instance, if we consider the subtable

$\mathrm{DT}_S([09], [03]) =$

	03	04	19	1E
09	4	·	4	·
0E	·	4	·	4
13	4	·	4	·
14	·	4	·	4

we can see that the sum of each row or column is equal to $8 = 2^2 \times \mathrm{DT}_{\rho'}(5, 3)$ since $L_V(5) =$ 09 and $L_V(3) =$ 03.

Finally, Theorem 3.16 ensures that the subtable $\mathrm{DT}_S(V, V) = \mathrm{DT}_S([00], [00])$ is the sum of the differential tables $(\mathrm{DT}_{\tau'_u})_{u \in U}$. ▲

ρ'

	0	1	2	3	4	5	6	7
0	8	.	.	.	.	.	.	.
1	.	.	2	2	2	2	.	.
2	.	.	.	.	2	2	2	2
3	.	.	2	2	.	.	2	2
4	.	2	2	.	2	.	.	2
5	.	2	.	2	.	2	.	2
6	.	2	2	.	.	2	2	.
7	.	2	.	2	2	.	2	.

$\mathcal{T}'_{00}$

	0	1	2	3
0	4	.	.	.
1	.	4	.	.
2	.	.	.	4
3	.	.	4	.

$\mathcal{T}'_{01}$

	0	1	2	3
0	4	.	.	.
1	.	.	.	4
2	.	.	4	.
3	.	4	.	.

$\mathcal{T}'_{02}$

	0	1	2	3
0	4	.	.	.
1	.	.	.	4
2	.	4	.	.
3	.	.	4	.

$\mathcal{T}'_{03}$

	0	1	2	3
0	4	.	.	.
1	.	.	.	4
2	.	.	4	.
3	.	4	.	.

$\mathcal{T}'_{08}$

	0	1	2	3
0	4	.	.	.
1	.	4	.	.
2	.	.	4	.
3	.	.	.	4

$\mathcal{T}'_{09}$

	0	1	2	3
0	4	.	.	.
1	.	.	4	.
2	.	4	.	.
3	.	.	.	4

$\mathcal{T}'_{0A}$

	0	1	2	3
0	4	.	.	.
1	.	.	4	.
2	.	.	.	4
3	.	4	.	.

$\mathcal{T}'_{0B}$

	0	1	2	3
0	4	.	.	.
1	.	4	.	.
2	.	.	.	4
3	.	.	4	.

		[00]				[01]				[02]				[03]				[08]				[09]				[0A]				[0B]			
		00	07	1A	1D	01	06	1B	1C	02	05	18	1F	03	04	19	1E	08	0F	12	15	09	0E	13	14	0A	0D	10	17	0B	0C	11	16
[00]	00	32	.	.	.	.	.	.	.	.	.	.	.	.	.	.	.	.	.	.	.	.	.	.	.	.	.	.	.	.	.	.	.
	07	.	12	8	12	.	.	.	.	.	.	.	.	.	.	.	.	.	.	.	.	.	.	.	.	.	.	.	.	.	.	.	.
	1A	.	8	12	12	.	.	.	.	.	.	.	.	.	.	.	.	.	.	.	.	.	.	.	.	.	.	.	.	.	.	.	.
	1D	.	12	12	8	.	.	.	.	.	.	.	.	.	.	.	.	.	.	.	.	.	.	.	.	.	.	.	.	.	.	.	.
[01]	01	.	.	.	.	.	.	.	.	.	4	4	.	4	.	.	4	2	2	2	2	.	4	4	.	.	.	.	.	.	.	.	.
	06	.	.	.	.	.	.	.	.	4	.	.	4	.	4	4	.	2	2	2	2	.	4	4	.	.	.	.	.	.	.	.	.
	1B	.	.	.	.	.	.	.	.	4	.	.	4	4	.	.	4	2	2	2	2	4	.	.	4	.	.	.	.	.	.	.	.
	1C	.	.	.	.	.	.	.	.	.	4	4	.	.	4	4	.	2	2	2	2	4	.	.	4	.	.	.	.	.	.	.	.
[02]	02	.	.	.	.	.	.	.	.	.	.	.	.	.	.	.	.	2	2	2	2	2	2	2	2	.	4	.	4	.	.	.	8
	05	.	.	.	.	.	.	.	.	.	.	.	.	.	.	.	.	2	2	2	2	2	2	2	2	4	.	4	.	8	.	.	.
	18	.	.	.	.	.	.	.	.	.	.	.	.	.	.	.	.	2	2	2	2	2	2	2	2	4	.	4	.	.	8	.	.
	1F	.	.	.	.	.	.	.	.	.	.	.	.	.	.	.	.	2	2	2	2	2	2	2	2	.	4	.	4	.	.	8	.
[03]	03	.	.	.	.	.	.	.	.	.	4	4	.	2	2	2	2	.	.	.	.	.	.	.	.	.	.	4	4	.	4	.	4
	04	.	.	.	.	.	.	.	.	.	4	4	.	2	2	2	2	.	.	.	.	.	.	.	.	.	.	4	4	.	4	.	4
	19	.	.	.	.	.	.	.	.	4	.	.	4	2	2	2	2	.	.	.	.	.	.	.	.	4	4	.	.	4	.	4	.
	1E	.	.	.	.	.	.	.	.	4	.	.	4	2	2	2	2	.	.	.	.	.	.	.	.	4	4	.	.	4	.	4	.
[08]	08	.	.	.	.	2	2	2	2	2	2	2	2	.	.	.	.	2	2	2	2	.	.	.	.	.	.	.	.	4	4	.	.
	0F	.	.	.	.	2	2	2	2	2	2	2	2	.	.	.	.	2	2	2	2	.	.	.	.	.	.	.	.	4	4	.	.
	12	.	.	.	.	2	2	2	2	2	2	2	2	.	.	.	.	2	2	2	2	.	.	.	.	.	.	.	.	.	.	4	4
	15	.	.	.	.	2	2	2	2	2	2	2	2	.	.	.	.	2	2	2	2	.	.	.	.	.	.	.	.	.	.	4	4
[09]	09	.	.	.	.	.	.	4	4	.	.	.	.	4	.	4	.	.	.	.	.	2	2	2	2	.	.	.	.	.	4	.	4
	0E	.	.	.	.	4	4	.	.	.	.	.	.	.	4	.	4	.	.	.	.	2	2	2	2	.	.	.	.	4	.	4	.
	13	.	.	.	.	4	4	.	.	.	.	.	.	4	.	4	.	.	.	.	.	2	2	2	2	.	.	.	.	4	.	4	.
	14	.	.	.	.	.	.	4	4	.	.	.	.	.	4	.	4	.	.	.	.	2	2	2	2	.	.	.	.	.	4	.	4
[0A]	0A	.	.	.	.	2	2	2	2	.	4	4	.	.	.	.	.	.	.	.	.	2	2	2	2	2	2	2	2	.	.	.	.
	0D	.	.	.	.	2	2	2	2	4	.	.	4	.	.	.	.	.	.	.	.	2	2	2	2	2	2	2	2	.	.	.	.
	10	.	.	.	.	2	2	2	2	.	4	4	.	.	.	.	.	.	.	.	.	2	2	2	2	2	2	2	2	.	.	.	.
	17	.	.	.	.	2	2	2	2	4	.	.	4	.	.	.	.	.	.	.	.	2	2	2	2	2	2	2	2	.	.	.	.
[0B]	0B	.	.	.	.	.	.	8	.	.	.	.	.	.	.	4	4	.	4	.	4	.	.	.	.	4	4	.	.	.	.	.	.
	0C	.	.	.	.	.	.	.	8	.	.	.	.	4	4	.	.	4	.	4	.	.	.	.	.	.	.	4	4	.	.	.	.
	11	.	.	.	.	.	8	.	.	.	.	.	.	.	.	4	4	.	4	.	4	.	.	.	.	.	.	4	4	.	.	.	.
	16	.	.	.	.	8	.	.	.	.	.	.	.	4	4	.	.	4	.	4	.	.	.	.	.	4	4	.	.	.	.	.	.

Figure 3.7. The reordered differential table of *S*.

http://dx.doi.org/10.5772/intechopen.70420

Corollary 3.18. The permutation S is at least δ-uniform for the differential cryptanalysis where δ denotes the even integer directly greater than or equal to $\frac{2^n}{2^d-1}$.

Example 3.19. In **Figure 3.7**, we can see that S is differentially 12-uniform. Thus, this S-box reaches the lower bound given by Corollary 3.18. ▲

3. The design of a trapdoor S-box

First, let us summarize the theorems of this section.

- Theorem 3.9 implies to reduce at most the linear uniformity of ρ' to keep the one of S as small as possible.
- In the same way, Theorem 3.15 implies to reduce at most the differential uniformity of ρ'.
- The same theorem also stresses that the greater the number of nonzero coefficients of $\mathrm{DT}_{\rho'}$ is, the better.
- Finally, Theorem 3.16 teaches us that the sum of the differential distribution tables $DT_{\tau'_u}$ should be as low as possible.

Now, to design the S-box S, one needs to pick a permutation ρ' of $\mathbb{F}_2^{n-d}$ with the smallest uniformities for linear and differential cryptanalysis. Then, one searches for permutations τ'_u of $\mathbb{F}_2^d$ satisfying the last condition. This search can be conducted randomly over every d-bit S-boxes. Finally, construct the S-box S as in the converse of Theorem 3.5. If the differential and linear uniformities of S are too far from the lower bounds given by Corollaries 3.12 and 3.18 and by Remark 3.13, then start again. In practice, these bounds are reached (or almost reached) after a small number of iterations.

Moreover, observe that the closer the dimension d of V from n is, the weaker the S-box S is against linear cryptanalysis and the stronger S is against differential cryptanalysis. The lower bounds given by Corollaries 3.12 and 3.18 and by Remark 3.13 are given in **Figure 3.8** for each $3 \le n \le 8$.

$n\backslash d$	1	2	3	4	5	6	7
3	4	4	.	.	.	.	.
4	4	8	8	.	.	.	.
5	8	8	16	16	.	.	.
6	8	16	16	32	32	.	.
7	12	16	32	32	64	64	.
8	16	23	32	64	64	128	128

$n\backslash d$	1	2	3	4	5	6	7
3	8	4	.	.	.	.	.
4	16	6	4	.	.	.	.
5	32	12	6	4	.	.	.
6	64	22	10	6	4	.	.
7	128	44	20	10	6	4	.
8	256	86	38	18	10	6	4

Figure 3.8. Lower bounds for the linear (left) and differential (right) uniformities of S.

Finally, it should be highlighted that these results can be used to easily prove that a given S-box does not map any linear partition to another one. For instance, the linear and differential uniformities of the S-box of Rijndeal [11] are far below the lower bounds given by Corollaries 3.12 and 3.18, no matter what the dimension d of the subspace V is. As a consequence, this S-box does not map any linear partition to another linear one.

http://dx.doi.org/10.5772/intechopen.70420

Backdoored Encryption Algorithm 1

BEA-1 [28] (*Backdoored Encryption Algorithm*) is an AES-like cipher together with a backdoor based on the theory developed in Chapters 2 and 3. This cipher is designed to resist linear and differential cryptanalysis. Nonetheless, the backdoor enables recovery of the full 120-bit cipher key in just a few seconds on a laptop computer using 2^{16} chosen plaintext blocks, as presented in [29].

This chapter is organized as follows. First, the specification of the cipher BEA-1 and its security analysis against linear and differential cryptanalysis are given in Section 1. Then, Section 2 explains the hidden property of the algorithm and its design. To conclude, the cryptanalysis exploiting the backdoor is detailed in Sections 3 and 4.

1. Presentation of BEA-1

The cipher BEA-1 is directly inspired by *Rijndael* [7], the block cipher designed by Joan Daemen and Vincent Rijmen, now known as the AES. Our algorithm encrypts 80-bit plaintext blocks using a 120-bit cipher key. Unlike the AES, the internal state is not seen as a matrix of bytes but as an array of 10-bit bundles. Therefore, the message and key spaces are respectively $(\mathbb{F}_2^{10})^8$ and $(\mathbb{F}_2^{10})^{12}$.

1.1. Specification of the encryption process

The encryption consists in applying 11 times a simple keyed operation called *round function* to the data block. A different 80-bit round key is used for each iteration of the round function. Since the last round is slightly different and uses two round keys, the encryption requires twelve 80-bit round keys. These round keys are derived from the 120-bit cipher key using a *key schedule*.

Like any other substitution-permutation network, the round function is made up of three stages: a *key addition*, a *substitution layer* and a *diffusion layer*.

- The key addition is just a bitwise "exclusive or" (XOR) between the data block and the round key.
- The substitution layer consists in the parallel evaluation of four different 10-bit S-boxes and is the only part of the cipher that is not affine. These S-boxes are referred to as S_0, S_1, S_2, S_3 and are defined in Figures 5A, 7A, 9A and 11A given in Appendix. They should not be confused with the secret S-boxes $\mathbf{S}_0$, $\mathbf{S}_1$, $\mathbf{S}_2$ and $\mathbf{S}_3$, only used in the design and the cryptanalysis of BEA-1.
- Following the design principles of the AES, the diffusion layer comes in two parts: the `ShiftRows` and the `MixColumns` operations. The first part is a bundle permutation. The

second evaluates in parallel the linear transformation $M : (\mathbb{F}_2^{10})^4 \to (\mathbb{F}_2^{10})^4$ processing four 10-bit bundles. Because of its linearity, M is only defined over the standard basis of $(\mathbb{F}_2^{10})^4$ in Figure 3A in Appendix. For convenience, its inverse M^{-1} is also in the same figure.

The pseudo-codes for the key schedule and the encryption algorithm are both given in **Figure 4.1.** To provide an overview of their structures, the first step of the key schedule and

Algorithm 1 - ExpandKey
Input. The 120-bit cipher key $K = (K_0, \ldots, K_{11}) \in (\mathbb{F}_2^{10})^{12}$.
Output. The twelve 80-bit round keys $k^{[0]}, \ldots, k^{[11]} \in (\mathbb{F}_2^{10})^8$.

$(k_0, \ldots, k_{11}) \leftarrow (K_0, \ldots, K_{11})$
For i **from** 0 **to** 6 **do**
  $x \leftarrow M(k_{12i+8}, \ldots, k_{12i+11})$
  $x \leftarrow (S_j(x_j))_{j<4}$
  $x \leftarrow (x_0 \oplus (3^i \bmod 2^{10}), x_1, x_2, x_3)$
  $(k_{12i+12}, \ldots, k_{12i+15}) \leftarrow (k_{12i+0}, \ldots, k_{12i+3}) \oplus x$
  $(k_{12i+16}, \ldots, k_{12i+19}) \leftarrow (k_{12i+4}, \ldots, k_{12i+7}) \oplus (k_{12i+12}, \ldots, k_{12i+15})$
  $(k_{12i+20}, \ldots, k_{12i+23}) \leftarrow (k_{12i+8}, \ldots, k_{12i+11}) \oplus (k_{12i+16}, \ldots, k_{12i+19})$
For r **from** 0 **to** 11 **do**
  $k^{[r]} \leftarrow (k_{8r+i})_{i<8}$
Return $k^{[0]}, \ldots, k^{[11]}$

Algorithm 2 - Encrypt
Input. The 120-bit master key $K \in (\mathbb{F}_2^{10})^{12}$ and the 80-bit plaintext block $p \in (\mathbb{F}_2^{10})^8$.
Output. The 80-bit ciphertext block $c \in (\mathbb{F}_2^{10})^8$.

$k^{[0]}, \ldots, k^{[11]} \leftarrow$ ExpandKey(K)
$x \leftarrow p$
For r **from** 0 **to** 9 **do**
  $x \leftarrow x \oplus k^{[r]}$ — *AddRoundKey*
  $x \leftarrow (S_{i \bmod 4}(x_i))_{i<8}$ — *SubBundles*
  $x \leftarrow (x_0, x_5, x_2, x_7, x_4, x_1, x_6, x_3)$ — *ShiftRows*
  $x \leftarrow (M \parallel M)(x)$ — *MixColumns*
$x \leftarrow x \oplus k^{[10]}$ — *AddRoundKey*
$x \leftarrow (S_{i \bmod 4}(x_i))_{i<8}$ — *SubBundles*
$x \leftarrow (x_0, x_5, x_2, x_7, x_4, x_1, x_6, x_3)$ — *ShiftRows*
$x \leftarrow x \oplus k^{[11]}$ — *AddRoundKey*
Return x

Figure 4.1. The key schedule and the encryption function of BEA-1.

the round function is illustrated in **Figure 4.2.** This representation also emphasizes the similarities between our algorithm and the AES.

Remark 4.1. The decryption is straightforward from the encryption since all the primitives are bijective. Thus, to decrypt, we just have to apply the inverse operations in the reverse order. It should be stressed that the key addition and the `ShiftRows` are involutions; therefore the same operations are used in the decryption process. Finally, note that the inverse S-boxes are not given here but can be computed by using the equation $S_i^{-1}(S(x)) = x$ holding for each x in $\mathbb{F}_2^{10}$.

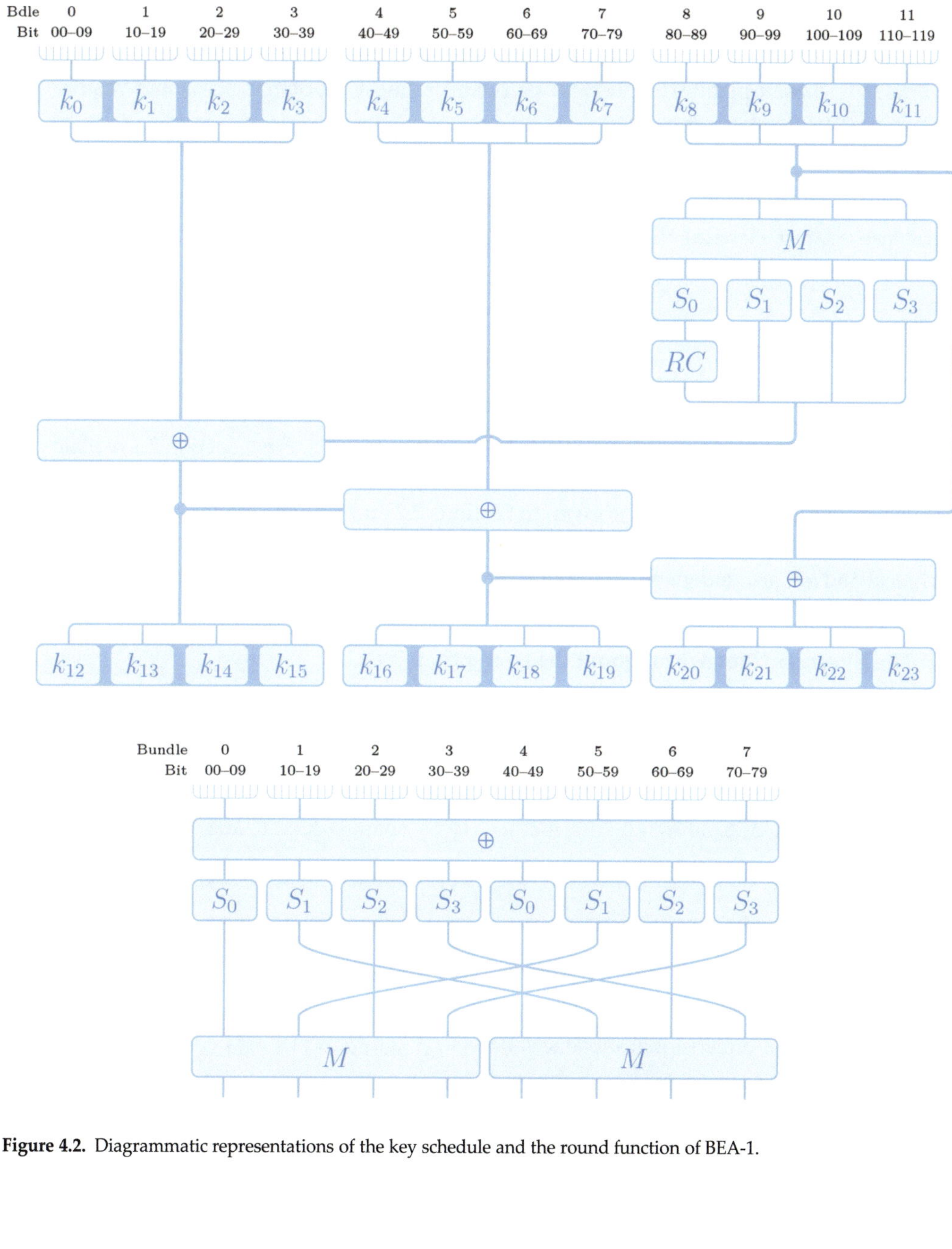

Figure 4.2. Diagrammatic representations of the key schedule and the round function of BEA-1.

1.2. Differential and linear cryptanalysis

In [7], Daemen and Rijmen introduced the differential and the linear branch numbers of a linear transformation. With an exhaustive search, it can be checked that the differential and linear branch numbers of M are both equal to 5, which is the maximum. This implies that any 2-round trail has at least 5 active S-boxes. Thus, a 10-round trail involves at least 25 active S-boxes.

Note that all the S-boxes are (at most) differentially 40-uniform and linearly 128-uniform. Therefore, the probability of any 10-round differential trail is upper bounded by $(\frac{40}{1024})^{25} \approx 2^{-116.9}$ and the absolute bias of a 10-round linear trail is upper bounded by $(\frac{128}{512})^{25} = 2^{-50}$. Consequently, a differential cryptanalysis of the 10-round version of our cipher would require at least 2^{117} chosen plaintext/ciphertext pairs and a linear cryptanalysis would require 2^{100} known plaintext/ciphertext pairs.

Even if this is a rough approximation since it does not take into account the inter-column diffusion provided by the `ShiftRows` operation, it suffices to prove the cipher's practical resistance against classical differential and linear cryptanalysis. In fact, there are only 2^{80} different plaintext/ciphertext pairs for a fixed cipher key.

2. Design of the backdoor

The presentation of secret structure of BEA-1 comes in two parts. First, Section 2.1 explains the nature of this backdoor and provides all the results needed to address the cryptanalysis. Then, the design of BEA-1's primitives is given in Sections 2.2 and 2.3. The reader who just wants to understand how the backdoor works can skip these two sections. Indeed, they are more technical and are also independent of the remainder of this chapter.

2.1. The linear partitions throughout the encryption

As said in introduction, the backdoor of BEA-1 relies on the theoretical framework developed in Chapters 2 and 3. Thus, it should not be surprising that linear partitions must play a key role in it. For this purpose, let us introduce the following 5-dimensional subspaces of $\mathbb{F}_2^{10}$

$$
\begin{aligned}
V_0 &= \mathrm{span}(\texttt{266}, \texttt{343}, \texttt{3ED}, \texttt{354}, \texttt{17F}), & W_0 &= \mathrm{span}(\texttt{16A}, \texttt{11B}, \texttt{306}, \texttt{05E}, \texttt{0B8}),\\
V_1 &= \mathrm{span}(\texttt{398}, \texttt{229}, \texttt{34C}, \texttt{251}, \texttt{37B}), & W_1 &= \mathrm{span}(\texttt{04B}, \texttt{3B7}, \texttt{0D5}, \texttt{027}, \texttt{2C8}),\\
V_2 &= \mathrm{span}(\texttt{0BA}, \texttt{155}, \texttt{307}, \texttt{37E}, \texttt{318}), & W_2 &= \mathrm{span}(\texttt{1A9}, \texttt{095}, \texttt{107}, \texttt{36F}, \texttt{2A3}),\\
V_3 &= \mathrm{span}(\texttt{1D1}, \texttt{21E}, \texttt{134}, \texttt{0DC}, \texttt{15A}), & W_3 &= \mathrm{span}(\texttt{0F0}, \texttt{2FE}, \texttt{191}, \texttt{332}, \texttt{1A6}).
\end{aligned}
$$

Then, define the 40-dimensional subspaces $V = \prod_{i=0}^{7} V_{i \bmod 4}$ and $W = \prod_{i=0}^{7} W_{i \bmod 4}$ of message space $(\mathbb{F}_2^{10})^8$. Therefore, the linear partitions $\mathcal{L}(V)$ and $\mathcal{L}(W)$ are both made up with 2^{40} cosets, each containing 2^{40} elements.

http://dx.doi.org/10.5772/intechopen.70420

The S-boxes S_0, S_1, S_2 and S_3 given in the specification of BEA-1 are actually derived from the *secret* S-boxes $\mathbf{S}_0$, $\mathbf{S}_1$, $\mathbf{S}_2$ and $\mathbf{S}_3$ given in Figures 4A, 6A, 8A and 10A in Appendix. The relation between the secret S-boxes $\mathbf{S}_i$ and their modified versions S_i will be detailed later in Section 2.2. In the first place, let us state the following theorem relating BEA-1 to the theory of partition-based backdoor ciphers.

Theorem 4.2. Consider the encryption function of BEA-1 where the *modified* S-boxes S_0, S_1, S_2, and S_3 are replaced with their *secret* counterparts $\mathbf{S}_0$, $\mathbf{S}_1$, $\mathbf{S}_2$, and $\mathbf{S}_3$. Then, the round function preserves the linear partition $\mathcal{L}(V)$ of $(\mathbb{F}_2^{10})^8$ and the last round maps $\mathcal{L}(V)$ to $\mathcal{L}(W)$, no matter the round keys used. As a consequence, the full encryption maps $\mathcal{L}(V)$ to $\mathcal{L}(W)$.

More precisely, **Figure 4.3** depicts the evolution of the linear partition $\mathcal{L}(V)$ throughout each primitive of the (secret) encryption process. For instance, we can see that the S-box $\mathbf{S}_i$ maps the linear partition $\mathcal{L}(V_i)$ to $\mathcal{L}(W_i)$, and hence, the substitution layer maps $\mathcal{L}(V)$ to $\mathcal{L}(W)$. Similarly, the diffusion layer comes back to the original partition, since it maps $\mathcal{L}(W)$ to $\mathcal{L}(V)$.

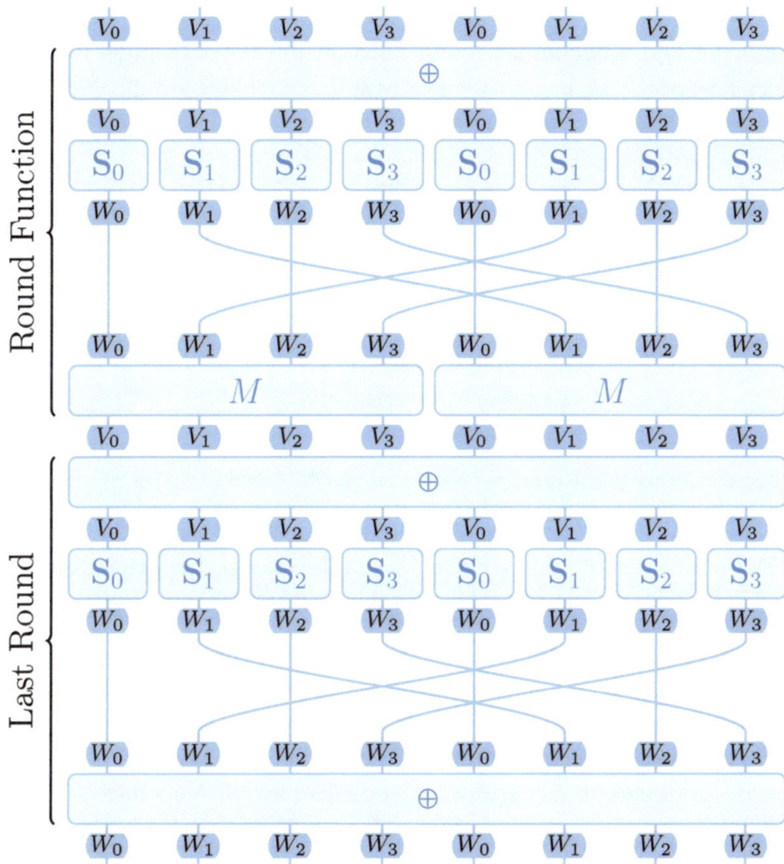

Figure 4.3. The linear partitions throughout the encryption.

Remark 4.3. Theorem 4.2, as well as Theorem 18 stated hereinafter, will be proven in Sections 2.2 and 2.3. Indeed, they establish the main properties of the backdoor and are hence closely related to the design of the cipher's primitives.

Thanks to Theorem 4.2, we can now explain our choices for the V_i and W_i. Each of these subspaces of $\mathbb{F}_2^{10}$ is a five-dimensional linear code whose minimal distance is equal to 4. This property ensures that the Hamming distance of any two different elements lying in the same coset is at least equal to 4. The subspaces V nd W of $\mathbb{F}_2^{80}$ inherit this property. Thus, if p is a plaintext, then any other plaintext p' lying in the same coset of V differs from p in at least four bits. Considering the secret encryption function, Theorem 4.2 establishes that their ciphertexts c and c' belong to the same coset of W. Thus, c and c' have at least four different bits. As it will become clear in the next two sections, the subspaces V_i and W_i could have been freely chosen among the five-dimensional subspaces of $\mathbb{F}_2^{10}$. We surmised that using linear codes with high minimal distance should reduce the likelihood of observing the backdoor by accident, hence our choice for the V_i and W_i.

Having explained the main property of the secret encryption function, now is the time to introduce the following theorem establishing a link between the secret cipher and BEA-1.

Theorem 4.4. Let $\mathbf{F}$ and $\mathbf{E}$ denote the round function and the encryption function of BEA-1 using the secret S-boxes. Let $p = p^{[0]}$ be any plaintext. Define the following elements with respect to the round keys $k^{[0]}, \ldots, k^{[10]}$:

$$p^{[i+1]} = F_{k^{[i]}}(p^{[i]}) \quad \text{and} \quad \mathbf{p}^{[i+1]} = \mathbf{F}_{k^{[i]}}(p^{[i]}) \quad \text{for } 0 \leq i < 11 .$$

Assume that the round keys $k^{[0]},\ldots,k^{[10]}$ are independent and uniformly distributed. The probability that all the equalities $p^{[i]} = \mathbf{p}^{[i]}$ hold for each $1 \leq i \leq 11$ is given by

$$\left(\left(\frac{944}{1024}\right)^6 \times \left(\frac{925}{1024}\right)^2\right)^{11} \approx 2^{-11} .$$

Therefore, the probability that p is encrypted equally with E and $\mathbf{E}$ can be approximated by 2^{-11}.

Remark 4.5. The fact that the `MixColumns` operation is replaced with a key addition in the last round of BEA-1 does not matter in Theorem 4.4. For the sake of simplicity, we then ignore this detail. This explains why the last round key $k^{[11]}$ does not appear in the statement of this result.

Needless to say, the hypothesis that the round keys are independent and uniformly distributed is mathematically wrong in any practical cryptanalysis. Indeed, the twelve 80-bit round keys are all extracted from one 120-bit cipher key. However, the cipher key needs to have (at least) 960 bits to provide independence and uniform distribution to its round keys. Such a cipher key must be related to the concept of long-key cipher defined in [30]. Nonetheless, if the cipher key is uniformly distributed, the same applies for each round key.

In our cryptanalysis of BEA-1, we are given plaintexts with their ciphertexts encrypted under a fixed cipher key. Even if we forget about the independence of the round keys, each plaintext must be encrypted with a random cipher key to make use of Theorem 4.4.

Fortunately, our experiments suggest that the proportion of the plaintexts encrypted equally with E_K and $\mathbf{E}_K$ is approximatively 2^{-11}, even when the round keys are derived from a fixed cipher key K. To put it another way, if $\mathcal{P}$ is a subset of the plaintext space $(\mathbb{F}_2^{10})^8$, it seems reasonable to assume that

$$\#\{p \in \mathcal{P} | E_K(p) = \mathbf{E}_K(p)\} \approx \frac{\#\mathcal{P}}{2^{11}} . \tag{4.1}$$

Now, suppose that $\mathcal{P}$ is included in a coset of V denoted by $x + V$. As the secret encryption function $\mathbf{E}_K$ maps $\mathcal{L}(V)$ to $\mathcal{L}(W)$ (see Theorem 4.2), we know that the image of $\mathcal{P}$ under $\mathbf{E}_K$ is included in a coset of W. More precisely, Lemma 2.8 establishes that $\mathbf{E}_K(\mathcal{P})$ is included in $y + W$ where $y = \mathbf{E}_K(x)$. Hence,

$$\{p \in \mathcal{P} | E_K(p) = \mathbf{E}_K(p)\} \subseteq \{p \in \mathcal{P} | E_K(p) \in (y + W)\} . \tag{4.2}$$

Combining (4.1) with (4.2), we conclude that approximately $\#\mathcal{P} \times 2^{-11}$ ciphertexts in $\mathcal{C} = E_k(\mathcal{P})$ belong to $y + W$. In addition, we have observed that the ciphertexts $c = E_K(p)$ such that $E_K(p) \neq \mathbf{E}_K(p)$ are spread over the 2^{40} cosets of W.

The backdoor of BEA-1 is hence the following. First, choose a set $\mathcal{P}$ of 2^{16} plaintexts uniformly chosen in one coset $x + V$ and collect their ciphertexts $\mathcal{C} = E_K(\mathcal{P})$ encrypted under an unknown cipher key K. Then search for the most represented coset of W in $\mathcal{C}$ and denote by y one of its representatives. According to our experiments, this coset should have roughly $2^{16-11} = 32$ elements, and the second most represented coset is unlikely to have more than six elements. As a consequence of the preceding discussion, we know that the coset $x + V$ is mapped to $y + W$ by the secret encryption function $\mathbf{E}_K$. This information can then be used to recover the cipher key K with a low computation cost, as detailed later in Sections 3 and 4.

To conclude this section, observe that no particular property of the key schedule has been used. It can be proven that each round of the key schedule preserves the linear partition $\mathcal{L}(\prod_{i=0}^{11} W_i)$, provided that the S-boxes S_i are replaced with their secret equivalents $\mathbf{S}_i$. This implies that if two cipher keys K and K' are in the same coset of $\prod_{i=0}^{11} W_i$, then we can approximate the probability that each pair of round keys $k^{[i]}$ and $k'^{[i]}$ are in the same coset of W by $(944^3 \cdot 925 \cdot 2^{-40})^7 \approx 2^{-3.5}$. However, for this property to be easily exploitable, the round keys ought to stay in the same coset of V instead of W (which can be simply achieved by switching the mappings M and $(S_0 \| S_1 \| S_2 \| S_3)$ in the key schedule). Therefore, if compared with our cryptanalysis, this property appears not to be very useful and was intentionally left as a wrong track.

2.2. The substitution layer

The nature of the hidden property of BEA-1 having been emphasized, this and the following sections detail the design of the cipher's primitives and prove Theorems 4.2 and 4.4 stated above. As explained in introduction, these two sections are aimed at the reader who wants to understand how BEA-1 was made. For a first read, it is possible to jump directly to Section 3 explaining the basic principle of the cryptanalysis using the backdoor.

Let {0*} and {*0} denote respectively the subspaces $\{0_5\} \times \mathbb{F}_2^5$ and $\mathbb{F}_2^5 \times \{0_5\}$ of $\mathbb{F}_2^{10}$. It should be noted that {*0} is a complement space of {0*} in $\mathbb{F}_2^{10}$. The design of each secret S-box $\mathbf{S}_i$ rests on a permutation $\mathbf{S}_i'$ of $\mathbb{F}_2^{10}$ preserving the linear partition $\mathcal{L}(\{0*\})$. Following Theorem 3.5, we just need to choose a permutation ρ_i of {*0} and a family $(\tau_{i,u})_{u\in\{*0\}}$ of permutations of {0*}. Then, we define $\mathbf{S}_i'$ for all $x = u + v$ in $\mathbb{F}_2^{10}$ by

$$\mathbf{S}_i'(x) = \mathbf{S}_i'(u+v) = \rho_i(u) + \tau_{i,u}(v),$$

where u is in {*0} and v in {0*}. The permutations ρ_i and $\tau_{i,u}$ were selected following the method given in Section 3, in order to maximize the resistance of $\mathbf{S}_i'$ against both differential and linear cryptanalysis.

Figure 1A in Appendix defines the linear mappings L_{V_i} and L_{W_i} (for $0 \le i \le 4$) over the standard basis of $\mathbb{F}_2^{10}$. It is worthwhile to note that these mappings are automorphisms of $\mathbb{F}_2^{10}$. Moreover, $L_{V_i}(\{0*\}) = V_i$ and $L_{W_i}(\{0*\}) = W_i$. By virtue of Proposition 2.15, we know that L_{V_i} maps $\mathcal{L}(\{0*\})$ to $\mathcal{L}(V_i)$ and that L_{W_i} maps $\mathcal{L}(\{0*\})$ to $\mathcal{L}(W_i)$. Last, but not least, define for each $0 \le i <$ 4 the secret S-box $\mathbf{S}_i$ by

$$\mathbf{S}_i = L_{W_i} \circ \mathbf{S'}_i \circ (L_{V_i})^{-1}.$$

These S-boxes are given in Figures 4A, 6A, 8A and 10A in Appendix. Obviously, $(L_{V_i})^{-1}$ maps $\mathcal{L}(V_i)$ to $\mathcal{L}(\{0*\})$, then $\mathbf{S'}_i$ preserves $\mathcal{L}(\{0*\})$, and L_{W_i} maps $\mathcal{L}(\{0*\})$ to $\mathcal{L}(W_i)$. This implies the following proposition.

Proposition 4.6. For each $0 \le i < 4$, the secret S-box $\mathbf{S}_i$ maps $\mathcal{L}(V_i)$ to $\mathcal{L}(W_i)$.

Remark 4.7. If the reader is interested in an explicit definition of the permutations ρ_i and the families of permutations $(\tau_{i,u})_{i\in\{*0\}}$, they can be recovered in the following way. First, compute $\mathbf{S'}_i = (L_{W_i})^{-1} \circ \mathbf{S}_i \circ L_{V_i}$ using the tables of Figures 1A and 4A (or 6A, 8A, 10A). As noted previously, the permutation $\mathbf{S'}_i$ preserves the linear partition $\mathcal{L}(\{0*\})$. To obtain its decomposition, we just have to follow the proof of Theorem 3.5. Thus, for each u in {*0}, define $\rho_i(u)$ as the unique element of $\{*0\} \cup (\mathbf{S'}_i(u) + \{0*\})$. It is not hard to see that $\rho_i(u)$ is simply equal to the element of $\mathbb{F}_2^{10}$, where the five leftmost bits are exactly the ones of $\mathbf{S'}_i(u)$ and the five remaining bits are all zero. Finally, for each u in {*0}, let $\tau_{i,u}$ be the permutation of {0*} defined by $\tau_{i,u}(v) = \mathbf{S'}_i(u+v) + \rho_i(u)$. Again, $\tau_{i,u}(v)$ is just the 10-bit vector having its five leftmost bits all zero and its five rightmost bits identical to the ones of $\mathbf{S'}_i(u+v)$. Naturally, the permutations ρ_i and $\tau_{i,u}$ can be seen as permutations of $\mathbb{F}_2^5$ (instead of {*0} and {0*}) to obtain the more convenient definition

$$\mathbf{S'}_i(u\|v) = (\rho_i(u)\|\tau_{i,u}(v)).$$

The modified S-boxes S_i given in the specification of BEA-1 are such that $S_i(x) = \mathbf{S}_i(x)$ for almost all input x in $\mathbb{F}_2^{10}$. For instance, $S_0(x) = \mathbf{S}_0(x)$ for all except 80 elements x in $\mathbb{F}_2^{10}$. The images of these 80 particular points are emphasized in Figures 4A and 5A. These modifications were chosen so as to improve the differential and linear resistances of S_0 compared to the original secret S-box $\mathbf{S}_0$. More generally, S_i and $\mathbf{S}_i$ have 80 different images for i in {0,1,2}. The last-modified S-box S_3 is less close to it secret equivalent since S_3 and $\mathbf{S}_3$ have 99 different images.

Consequently, if x is uniformly distributed over $\mathbb{F}_2^{10}$, then the equality $S_i(x) = \mathbf{S}_i(x)$ holds with probability q_i where

$$q_0 = q_1 = q_2 = \frac{944}{1024} \quad \text{and} \quad q_3 = \frac{925}{1024}.$$

This implies that when x is uniformly distributed over $(\mathbb{F}_2^{10})^8$, the images of x under the secret and the modified substitution layers are equal with probability $q = \left(\prod_{i=0}^{3} q_i\right)^2$.

Let $p = p^{[0]}$ be a plaintext. In the following, we use the notations of Theorem 4.4. If $k^{[i]}$ is uniformly distributed, then so is $p^{[i]} + k^{[i]}$. Thus, $p^{[i+1]} = F_{k^{[i]}}(p^{[i]})$ is equal to $\mathbf{p}^{[i+1]} = \mathbf{F}_{k^{[i]}}(p^{[i]})$ with probability q. Assuming moreover that the round keys are independent implies that the events $p^{[i]} = \mathbf{p}^{[i]}$ for each $1 \le i \le 11$ are independent. Therefore, the probability that the equalities $p^{[i]} = \mathbf{p}^{[i]}$ hold for all $1 \le i \le 11$ is given by q^{11}. This discussion proves Theorem 4.4.

2.3. The diffusion layer

Some components used to design the linear transformation M are defined over the finite field $\mathbb{F}_{2^5}$. In order to have an explicit construction of this field, we consider the irreducible polynomial $X^5 + X^2 + 1$ over $\mathbb{F}_2$ and define $\mathbb{F}_{2^5}$ as the quotient ring $\mathbb{F}_2[X]/(X^5 + X^2 + 1)$. Let α denote the equivalence class of X in $\mathbb{F}_{2^5}$. By construction, the equality $\alpha^5 + \alpha^2 + 1 = 0$ holds, or equivalently, $\alpha^5 = \alpha^2 + 1$. Each element of $\mathbb{F}_{2^5}$ can hence be uniquely written as $\sum_{i=0}^{4} x_i \alpha^i$ where $(x_4,\ldots, x_0)$ belongs to $\mathbb{F}_2^5$. More precisely, the family $(\alpha^i)_{i<5}$ is a basis of $\mathbb{F}_{2^5}$ seen as a 5-dimensional vector space over $\mathbb{F}_2$. The field $\mathbb{F}_{2^5}$ will then be identified with $(\mathbb{F}_2)^5$ via the isomorphism from $\mathbb{F}_2^5$ to $\mathbb{F}_{2^5}$ mapping $(x_4,\ldots, x_0)$ to $\sum_{i=0}^{4} x_i \alpha^i$. For instance, the element $\alpha^2 + \alpha + 1$ in $\mathbb{F}_{2^5}$ is identified with 07 in $\mathbb{F}_2^5$. Now define the 4×4 matrices M_U and M_V over $\mathbb{F}_{2^5}$ by

$$\begin{pmatrix} a & b & c & d \\ b & a & d & c \\ c & d & a & b \\ d & c & b & a \end{pmatrix} \qquad M_U : \begin{cases} a = \alpha^4 + \alpha^2, \\ b = \alpha^4 + \alpha^3 + \alpha^2 + \alpha + 1, \\ c = \alpha^3 + \alpha^2, \\ d = \alpha^4 + \alpha^2 + 1, \end{cases} \qquad M_V : \begin{cases} a = \alpha^3 + \alpha^2 + 1, \\ b = \alpha^4 + \alpha^3 + \alpha^2 + \alpha, \\ c = \alpha^4 + \alpha^2 + \alpha \\ d = \alpha^3. \end{cases}$$

It can be verified that these matrices are MDS. In other words, the [8, 4]-linear code having $G = [\mathrm{Id}_4, M_U]$ as generator matrix has minimal distance equals to 5, which is the maximum achievable.

Each of these matrices naturally induces an automorphism of $(\mathbb{F}_{2^5})^4$ and hence of $(\mathbb{F}_2^{10})^4$. For instance, M_U maps the element $x = (x_0, x_1, x_2, x_3)$ to $x \times M_U$. Observe that we chose to see elements of $(\mathbb{F}_2^{10})^4$ as row vectors to keep the common notations of linear codes.

Example 4.8. To illustrate these notations, let us compute the image of the element $x = (\texttt{00}, \texttt{02}, \texttt{00}, \texttt{00})$ of $(\mathbb{F}_2^{10})^4$ under the automorphism induced by M_U. First, x is identified with the element $(0, \alpha, 0, 0)$ of $(\mathbb{F}_{2^5})^4$. Then,

$$\begin{aligned}(0,\alpha,0,0) \times M_U &= (\alpha(\alpha^4+\alpha^3+\alpha^2+\alpha+1), \alpha(\alpha^4+\alpha^2), \alpha(\alpha^4+\alpha^2+1), \alpha(\alpha^3+\alpha^2)) \\ &= (\alpha^5+\alpha^4+\alpha^3+\alpha^2+\alpha, \quad \alpha^5+\alpha^3, \quad \alpha^5+\alpha^3+\alpha, \quad \alpha^4+\alpha^3) \\ &= (\alpha^4+\alpha^3+\alpha+1, \alpha^3+\alpha^2+1, \alpha^3+\alpha^2+\alpha+1, \qquad \alpha^4+\alpha^3).\end{aligned}$$

Therefore, $(\texttt{00}, \texttt{02}, \texttt{00}, \texttt{00}) \times M_U = (\texttt{1B}, \texttt{0D}, \texttt{0F}, \texttt{18})$. ▲

As was the case for the secret S-boxes $\mathbf{S}_i$, the linear transformation M rests upon the linear transformation M' defined as follows

$$\begin{aligned} M' : (\mathbb{F}_2^{10})^4 &\rightarrow (\mathbb{F}_2^{10})^4 \\ (u_i \parallel v_i)_{i<4} &\mapsto (\rho(u)_i \parallel \tau_u(v)_i)_{i<4} \end{aligned}$$

where $\rho(u) = u \times M_U$ and $\tau_u(v) = v \times M_V + P_{U\rightarrow V}(u)$. The strength of this construction is that M' inherits the linear and differential branch numbers of M_U and M_V, as stated in the proposition hereunder. But first, we introduce the following example.

Example 4.9. Let us compute the image of $x = (\texttt{000}, \texttt{070}, \texttt{000}, \texttt{000})$ under M'. As a first step, observe that x can be written as

$$x = (\texttt{00}\|\texttt{00}, \texttt{03}\|\texttt{10}, \texttt{00}\|\texttt{00}, \texttt{00}\|\texttt{00}) = (u_i\|v_i)_{i<4},$$

where $u = (\texttt{00}, \texttt{03}, \texttt{00}, \texttt{00})$ and $v = (\texttt{00}, \texttt{10}, \texttt{00}, \texttt{00})$. Let $e_9 = (\texttt{00}, \texttt{02}, \texttt{00}, \texttt{00})$ and $e_{10} = (\texttt{00}, \texttt{01}, \texttt{00}, \texttt{00})$. Then $u = e_9 + e_{10}$, it is indeed its decomposition over the standard basis of $(\mathbb{F}_2^5)^4$. Thus, for any linear mapping L, it holds that $L(u) = L(e_9) + L(e_{10})$. The image of u under ρ can hence be computed by

$$\rho(u) = \rho(e_9) + \rho(e_{10}) = (\texttt{1B}, \texttt{0D}, \texttt{0F}, \texttt{18}) + (\texttt{1F}, \texttt{14}, \texttt{15}, \texttt{0C}) = (\texttt{04}, \texttt{19}, \texttt{1A}, \texttt{14}).$$

In the same way,

$$\begin{aligned}\tau_u(v) &= v \times M_V + P_{U\rightarrow V}(e_9) + P_{U\rightarrow V}(e_{10}) \\ &= (\texttt{16}, \texttt{0E}, \texttt{14}, \texttt{02}) + (\texttt{0F}, \texttt{11}, \texttt{0C}, \texttt{16}) + (\texttt{11}, \texttt{0E}, \texttt{02}, \texttt{0A}) = (\texttt{08}, \texttt{11}, \texttt{1A}, \texttt{1E}).\end{aligned}$$

Consequently, $M'(x) = (\texttt{04} \parallel \texttt{08}, \texttt{19} \parallel \texttt{11}, \texttt{1A} \parallel \texttt{1A}, \texttt{14} \parallel \texttt{1E}) = (\texttt{088}, \texttt{331}, \texttt{35A}, \texttt{29E})$. ▲

Proposition 4.10. The linear and the differential branch numbers of M' are both equal to 5. Thus, M' is a perfect diffusion layer.

Proof. Let $x = (u_i \parallel v_i)_{i<4}$ be a nonzero element of $(\mathbb{F}_2^{10})^4$. In order to prove that the differential branch number of M' is equal to 5, we need to show that $\mathrm{w}_{10}(x) + \mathrm{w}_{10}(M'(x))$ is greater than or equal to 5. First, assume that $u = (u_i)_{i<4}$ is nonzero. Using the fact that M_U is MDS, we obtain the inequality $\mathrm{w}_5(u) + \mathrm{w}_5(u \times M_U) \geq 5$. Next,

$$5 \le w_5(u) + w_5(\rho(u)) = w_{10}((u_i \parallel 0)_{i<4}) + w_{10}((\rho(u)_i \parallel 0)_{i<4})$$
$$\le w_{10}((u_i \parallel v_i)_{i<4}) + w_{10}((\rho((u)_i \parallel \tau_u(v)_i)_{i<4}) = w_{10}(x) + w_{10}(M'(x)).$$

Now, suppose that $u = 0$. It must be the case that $v \neq 0$ as x is nonzero by definition. Again, it holds that $w_5(v) + w_5(v \times M_V) \ge 5$ because M_V is also MDS. Then,

$$5 \le w_5(v) + w_5(\tau_0(v)) = w_{10}((0 \parallel v_i)_{i<4}) + w_{10}((0 \parallel \tau_0(v)_i)_{i<4})$$
$$= w_{10}(x) + w_{10}(M'(x)).$$

We have proven that $w_{10}(x) + w_{10}(M'(x)) \ge 5$ for any nonzero element x of $(\mathbb{F}_2^{10})^4$. Consequently, the differential branch number of M' is greater than or equal to 5. The equality $\mathcal{B}_D(M') = 5$ follows as 5 is the maximum achievable. Similarly, it can be proven that M' has also the maximum linear branch number. It follows that M' is a perfect diffusion layer and the result is proven. ▪

Recall that the notation {0*} denotes the subspace $\{0_5\} \times \mathbb{F}_2^5$ and that the linear mappings L_{V_i} and L_{W_i} (see Figure 1A) map respectively $\mathcal{L}(\{0*\})$ to $\mathcal{L}(V_i)$ and $\mathcal{L}(\{0*\})$ to $\mathcal{L}(W_i)$. It is then easily seen that M' maps $\{0^*\}^4$ to itself. Thus, M' preserves the partition $\mathcal{L}(\{0*\}^4)$ by Proposition 2.15. Finally, define

$$M = (L_{V_0} \parallel L_{V_1} \parallel L_{V_2} \parallel L_{V_3}) \circ M' \circ (L_{W_0} \parallel L_{W_1} \parallel L_{W_2} \parallel L_{W_3})^{-1}.$$

From its definition, it is straightforward to check that M maps the linear partition $\mathcal{L}(\prod_{i=0}^{3} W_i)$ to $\mathcal{L}(\prod_{i=0}^{3} V_i)$.

Example 4.11. We are going to compute M(000, 080, 000, 000). First, we have that

$$(L_{W_0} \parallel L_{W_1} \parallel L_{W_2} \parallel L_{W_3})^{-1}(\texttt{000}, \texttt{080}, \texttt{000}, \texttt{000})$$
$$= (L_{W_0}^{-1}(\texttt{000}), L_{W_1}^{-1}(\texttt{080}), L_{W_2}^{-1}(\texttt{000}), L_{W_3}^{-1}(\texttt{000})) = (\texttt{000}, \texttt{070}, \texttt{000}, \texttt{000}).$$

Then, the image of (000, 070, 000, 000) under M' is (088, 331, 35A, 29E), as already established in Example 4.9. Finally,

$$M(\texttt{000}, \texttt{080}, \texttt{000}, \texttt{000}) = (L_{V_0} \parallel L_{V_1} \parallel L_{V_2} \parallel L_{V_3})(\texttt{088}, \texttt{331}, \texttt{35A}, \texttt{29E})$$
$$= (\texttt{15E}, \texttt{0BF}, \texttt{1E2}, \texttt{04F}).$$

Indeed, $L_{V_0}(\texttt{088}) = L_{V_0}(\texttt{080}) + L_{V_0}(\texttt{008}) = \texttt{21D} + \texttt{343} = \texttt{15E}$. The three other bundles are computed in the same manner. ▲

Because each mapping L_{V_i} or L_{W_i} operates on different bundles and is invertible, it is clear that the linear and differential branch numbers of M are the same as M'. This discussion completes the proof of the following corollary.

Corollary 4.12. The linear mapping M is a perfect diffusion layer, which maps $\mathcal{L}(\prod_{i=0}^{3} W_i)$ to $\mathcal{L}(\prod_{i=0}^{3} V_i)$.

In conclusion, Proposition 2.13 ensures that any key addition preserves all the linear partitions, and hence it preserves $\mathcal{L}(V)$. Next, it has been proven in Section 2.2 that every secret S-box $\mathbf{S}_i$ maps $\mathcal{L}(V_i)$ to $\mathcal{L}(W_i)$. Thus, the secret substitution layer maps $\mathcal{L}(V)$ to $\mathcal{L}(W)$. It is clear that the `ShiftRows` operation is linear and maps W to itself. According to Proposition 2.15, this mapping preserves $\mathcal{L}(W)$. Finally, the `MixColumn` operation maps $\mathcal{L}(W)$ to $\mathcal{L}(V)$ by Corollary 4.12. This discussion is summarized in **Figure 4.3** and proves Theorem 4.2 previously given in Section 2.1.

3. Main idea of the cryptanalysis

As we have seen in Section 2.1, the cipher BEA-1 does not map a linear partition to another one but behaves as though it did for a nonnegligible fraction of the message space. This nontrivial property can be used to recover the cipher key in an operational cryptanalysis. But before considering the full cipher, we give the main idea of this attack.

3.1. A detailed example

To explain how to take advantage of this backdoor, we introduce a toy example. First, let us mention that all the notations of this section are independent of the remainder of this chapter. The message space of this toy cipher is simply $\mathbb{F}_2^6$. Then, consider the subspaces V and W of $\mathbb{F}_2^6$ defined by

$$V = \text{span}(01, 02, 10, 20) = \{(x_3, x_2, 0, 0, x_1, x_0) | x \in \mathbb{F}_2^4\},$$
$$W = \text{span}(01, 02, 04, 10) = \{(0, x_3, 0, x_2, x_1, x_0) | x \in \mathbb{F}_2^4\}.$$

Thus, $\mathcal{L}(V) = \{x + V | x \in \{00, 04, 08, 0C\}\}$ and $\mathcal{L}(W) = \{y + W | y \in \{00, 08, 20, 28\}\}$.

Let $\mathbf{S}$ be the permutation of $\mathbb{F}_2^6$ given in **Figure 4.4.** We defined another permutation S of $\mathbb{F}_2^6$ satisfying $S(x) = \mathbf{S}(x)$ for any input x in $\mathbb{F}_2^6$ except 00, 01, 04, 05, 08, 09, 0C and 0D. The images of these eight specific points under S are also given in **Figure 4.4.** By analogy with Section 2, the permutation $\mathbf{S}$ represents the *secret* S-box used to design the trapdoor whereas S represents the *modified* S-box given in the specification of the algorithm. Lastly, define the following keyed mappings

		.0	.1	.2	.3	.4	.5	.6	.7	.8	.9	.A	.B	.C	.D	.E	.F
$\mathbf{S}(x)$	0.	1C	1E	1F	08	39	3A	3C	2A	13	05	02	03	37	20	24	31
	1.	0D	18	0A	1A	3B	2D	29	3E	14	07	11	10	25	26	21	35
	2.	1B	19	0B	1D	2B	2F	2C	28	15	01	16	06	27	36	30	32
	3.	0C	09	0F	0E	3F	2E	3D	38	00	17	04	12	22	23	33	34
$S(x)$	0.	39	05			13	1C			37	20			1E	3A		

Figure 4.4. The theoretical and the modified S-boxes.

$$\mathbf{F}_k : \mathbb{F}_2^6 \to \mathbb{F}_2^6 \qquad\qquad F_k : \mathbb{F}_2^6 \to \mathbb{F}_2^6$$
$$x \mapsto \mathbf{S}(x) + k, \qquad\qquad x \mapsto S(x) + k,$$

representing respectively the secret and the modified round functions. Naturally, the key k can be any element of $\mathbb{F}_2^6$.

It can be easily verified that the secret S-box $\mathbf{S}$ maps $\mathcal{L}(V)$ to $\mathcal{L}(W)$. In fact, we have that

$$\mathbf{S}(\mathtt{00} + V) = \mathtt{08} + W, \qquad \mathbf{S}(\mathtt{08} + V) = \mathtt{00} + W,$$
$$\mathbf{S}(\mathtt{04} + V) = \mathtt{28} + W, \qquad \mathbf{S}(\mathtt{0C} + V) = \mathtt{20} + W.$$

In contrast with the secret permutation $\mathbf{S}$, the modified S-box S does not map $\mathcal{L}(V)$ to $\mathcal{L}(W)$. However, the equality $S(x) = \mathbf{S}(x)$ holds with probability $^{56}/_{64}$ assuming that x is uniformly distributed over $\mathbb{F}_2^6$. This can be stated equivalently as

$$\#\{x \in \mathbb{F}_2^6 | S(x) = \mathbf{S}(x)\} = 2^6 - 8 = 56 .$$

It should also be noted that this statement remains valid when considering their inverse mappings, that is $\#\{y \in \mathbb{F}_2^6 \mid S^{-1}(y) = \mathbf{S}^{-1}(y)\} = 56$. Indeed, if x is an element of $\mathbb{F}_2^6$ such that $S(x) = \mathbf{S}(x)$, then $y = S(x)$ satisfies the equality $S^{-1}(x) = \mathbf{S}^{-1}(y)$. As a consequence,

$$\#\{x \in \mathbb{F}_2^6 | S(x) = \mathbf{S}(x)\} \le \#\{y \in \mathbb{F}_2^6 \mid S^{-1}(y) = \mathbf{S}^{-1}(y)\} .$$

The converse inequality can be proven in the same way, establishing the equality.

Now, consider the subset $\mathcal{P}$ of $\mathbb{F}_2^6$ defined hereinafter. We assume that the round key is $k = \mathtt{37}$. The image of $\mathcal{P}$ under $\mathbf{S}$ and its encryption with $\mathbf{F}_{37}$ are given below.

$$\begin{aligned}
\mathcal{P} &= \{ \overbrace{\mathtt{22}}^{\in(\mathtt{00}+V)} , \overbrace{\mathtt{04, 05, 06, 15, 16, 17, 27, 34, 35, 36}}^{\in(\mathtt{04}+V)} , \overbrace{\mathtt{18, 3A}}^{\in(\mathtt{08}+V)} , \overbrace{\mathtt{0D, 0F}}^{\in(\mathtt{0C}+V)} \},\\
\mathbf{S}(\mathcal{P}) &= \{ \mathtt{0B} , \mathtt{39, 3A, 3C, 2D, 29, 3E, 28, 3F, 2E, 3D} , \mathtt{14, 04} , \mathtt{20, 31} \},\\
\mathbf{F}_{37}(\mathcal{P}) &= \{ \underbrace{\mathtt{3C}}_{\in(\mathtt{28}+W)} , \underbrace{\mathtt{0E, 0D, 0B, 1A, 1E, 09, 1F, 08, 19, 0A}}_{\in(\mathtt{08}+W)} , \underbrace{\mathtt{23, 33}}_{\in(\mathtt{20}+W)} , \underbrace{\mathtt{17, 06}}_{\in(\mathtt{00}+W)} \}.
\end{aligned}$$

It should be stressed that the coset $\mathtt{04} + V$ is significantly more represented in $\mathcal{P}$ than any other coset of V. Since $\mathbf{F}_{37}(\mathcal{P})$ maps the linear partition $\mathcal{L}(V)$ to $\mathcal{L}(W)$, the messages belonging to the same coset of V are all mapped to the same coset of W. Therefore, the most represented coset of W in $\mathbf{F}_{37}(\mathcal{P})$ has also ten elements.

As we have seen above, the modified round function F_{37} does not map $\mathcal{L}(V)$ to $\mathcal{L}(W)$. **Figure 4.5** displays the differences between the encryption of $\mathcal{P}$ with $\mathbf{F}_{37}$ and its encryption with F_{37} by highlighting the messages x in P such that $S(x) \neq \mathbf{S}(x)$ (that is $\mathtt{04}$, $\mathtt{05}$, and $\mathtt{0D}$) and their images throughout the encryption.

To explain these differences, let us first consider the set $\mathcal{Q}$ of the ten messages lying in both $\mathcal{P}$ and 04 + V. Knowing that the equality $S(x) = \mathbf{S}(x)$ holds with probability $^{56}/_{64}$ when x is uniformly distributed, it seems reasonable to assume that only $10\times^{56}/_{64} = 8.75$ messages of $\mathcal{Q}$ will remain in the same coset when computing their images under S. By comparing with the actual messages in $\mathcal{Q}$, we can see that this is a good approximation since eight messages in $S(\mathcal{Q})$ belong to the same coset of W.

$$\mathcal{Q} = \{\, \mathtt{04}, \mathtt{05}\,,\ \mathtt{06}, \mathtt{15}, \mathtt{16}, \mathtt{17}, \mathtt{27}, \mathtt{34}, \mathtt{35}, \mathtt{36}\,\} = \mathcal{P} \cap (\mathtt{04} + V),$$
$$S(\mathcal{Q}) = \{\, \underbrace{\mathtt{13}, \mathtt{1C}}_{\notin (\mathtt{28}+W)}\,,\ \underbrace{\mathtt{3C}, \mathtt{2D}, \mathtt{29}, \mathtt{3E}, \mathtt{28}, \mathtt{3F}, \mathtt{2E}, \mathtt{3D}}_{\in (\mathtt{28}+W)}\,\}.$$

Needless to say, there are also eight messages in $F_{37}(\mathcal{Q})$ lying in the same coset of W because the key addition preserves $\mathcal{L}(W)$.

We focus now to the set $\mathcal{P}$ as a whole. According to the discussion above, we know that the most represented coset of W in $F_{37}(\mathcal{P})$ has at least eight elements. We have seen that the images under S of messages lying in the same coset may not stay together. Nonetheless, the converse can also be true, and messages in different cosets may end up in the same coset. This is exactly what happens with the message 0D, as illustrated in **Figure 4.5.** Consequently, the most represented coset in $F_{37}(\mathcal{P})$ has actually nine elements.

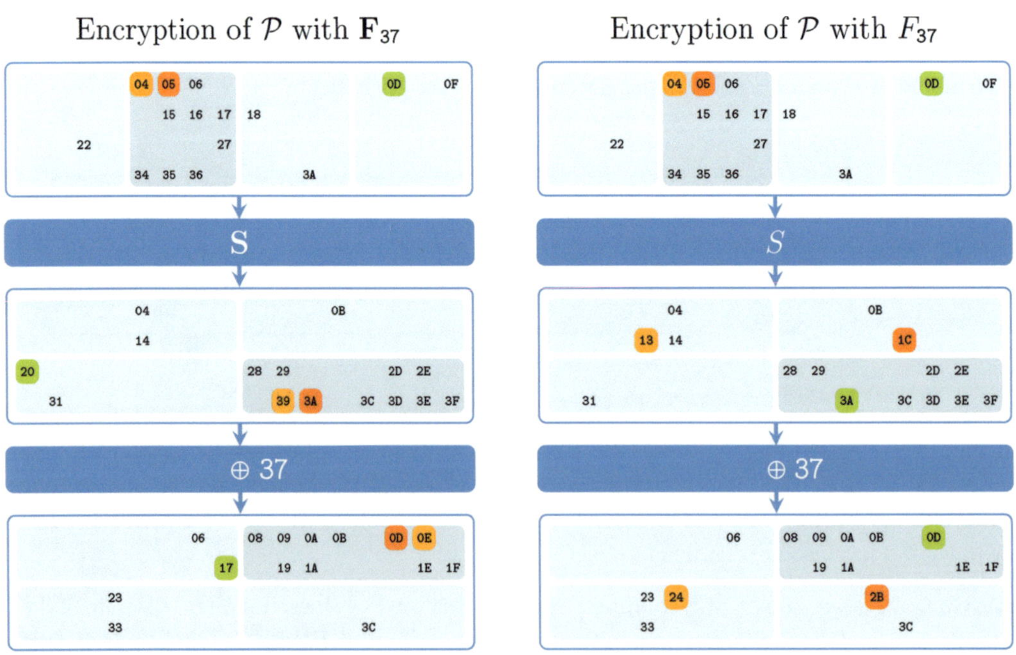

Figure 4.5. Encryption with $\mathbf{F}_{37}$ and F_{37}.

http://dx.doi.org/10.5772/intechopen.70420

The fact that the most represented coset may not only lose but occasionally retrieve elements should be seen as a side effect. Its impact remains low when

- one coset has significantly more elements than all other cosets (say at least 5 times more), and
- when the number of messages is lower than the total number of cosets.

We must nevertheless keep this fact in mind to understand why the right key will not necessarily have the best score.

It is now time to explain how to recover the round key using only the set $\mathcal{C} = F_{37}(\mathcal{P})$ of encrypted messages. First, we have to determine the most represented coset in $\mathcal{C}$. In our example, this coset is 08 + W with nine messages, and u = 08 is one of its representatives.

Now, assume that k is the round key used to encrypt $\mathcal{C}$. We need to find the coset of V which is mapped to $\mathbf{u} + W$ by the secret round function $\mathbf{F}_k$. According to Lemma 2.8, F_k maps $\mathbf{t} + V$ to $\mathbf{F}_k(\mathbf{t}) + W$. A representative of this coset of V is then $\mathbf{t} = \mathbf{S}^{-1}(\mathbf{u} + k)$. Finally, the *score* of the guessed key k is the number of messages $F_k^{-1}(c) = S^{-1}(c + k)$ that belong to the theoretical coset $\mathbf{t} + V$, that is to say

$$\mathrm{score}(k) = \#\{c \in C | S^{-1}(c + k) \in (\mathbf{t} + V)\}.$$

Figure 4.6 illustrates the scoring process applied to the right key (37) and to a wrong key (07). We naturally recover the set $\mathcal{P}$ and the coset $\mathbf{t} + V = 34 + V = 04 + V$ when using the right

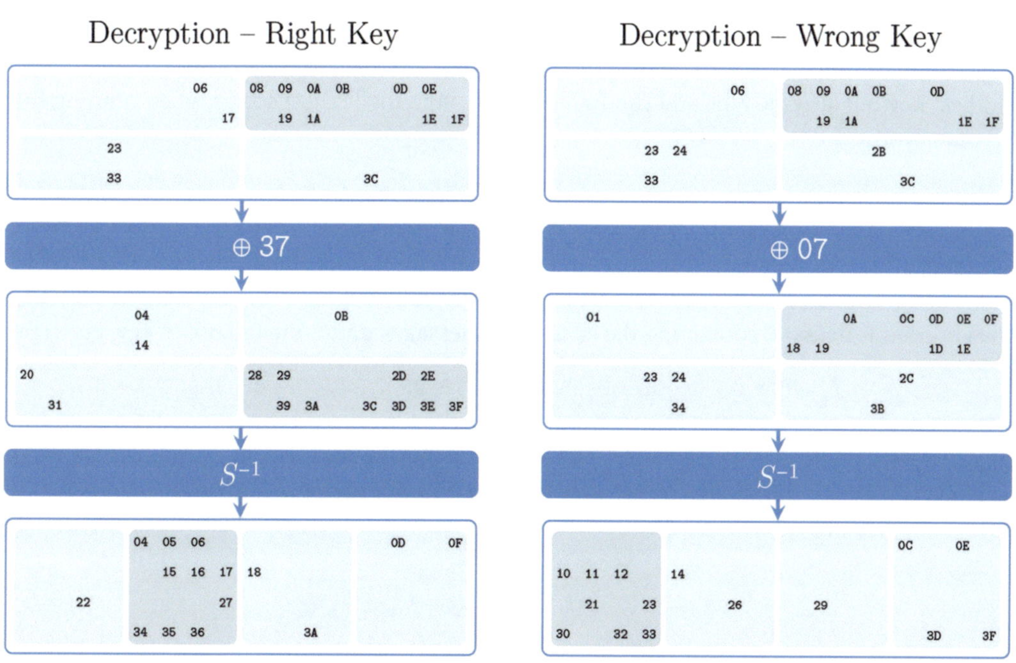

Figure 4.6. Decryption with the right key and with a wrong key.

Key	0B	12	1C	37	03	05	10	1D	20	21	22	2C	2F	35	36	38
Score	11	10	10	10	9	9	9	9	9	9	9	9	9	9	9	9
Key	3B	3C	3D	00	01	02	04	06	07	08	09	0A	0E	0F	11	13
Score	9	9	9	8	8	8	8	8	8	8	8	8	8	8	8	8
Key	18	19	1E	1F	24	25	26	27	2A	2B	2D	2E	30	34	39	3A
Score	8	8	8	8	8	8	8	8	8	8	8	8	8	8	8	8
Key	0C	0D	14	15	16	17	1A	1B	23	28	29	31	32	33	3E	3F
Score	7	7	7	7	7	7	7	7	7	7	7	7	7	7	7	7

Figure 4.7. The scores for each key.

key. Thus, the score of $k = 37$ is equal to 10. In the same way, the score of $k = 07$ is the number of decrypted messages in the coset $\mathbf{t} + V = 32 + V = 00 + V$, so $\text{score}(07) = 8$.

Let us now explain why a wrong key tends to have a lower score than the right key. First, the addition of the wrong key randomizes the cosets and the messages within. Recall that when the input x is uniformly distributed, the equality $S^{-1}(x) = \mathbf{S}^{-1}(x)$ holds with probability $^{56}/_{64}$. The most represented coset after the addition of the wrong key should then lose some elements by applying S^{-1}. Thus, the score of any wrong key should be lower than or equal to 8.

It goes without saying that the previous discussion gives just the main idea of the cryptanalysis. For some wrong keys, the side effects are significant, and their scores can even be higher than the score of the right key, as shown in **Figure 4.7.** Indeed, the key 37 is one the four best keys but is not the one that has the highest score (0B). For this reason, we will not only return the best key but also the NbCand candidate keys having the highest scores when running this cryptanalysis.

3.2. Formalization of the attack

The aim of this section is to formalize and to generalize the cryptanalysis introduced previously in Section 3.1. As we have just seen, this attack really begins in **Figure 4.6.** The very first data needed is the set C containing the encrypted messages under the unknown key, given by

$$C = \{04, 05, 06, 0D, 0F, 15, 16, 17, 18, 22, 27, 34, 35, 36, 3A\}.$$

Naturally, C is included in the set $\mathscr{C} = \mathbb{F}_2^6$ of all possible ciphertexts. Similarly, the set of all possible round keys is denoted by $\mathscr{K} = \mathbb{F}_2^6$. Next, define the keyed mapping

$$\begin{aligned} G : \mathscr{K} \times \mathscr{C} &\to \mathbb{F}_2^6 \\ (k, c) &\mapsto S^{-1}(c + k). \end{aligned}$$

Each mapping $G_k : c \mapsto G(k, c)$ is the inverse of the round function F_k. The secret counterpart of G is $\mathbf{G} : (k, c) \mapsto \mathbf{S}^{-1}(c + k)$. Observe that for each round key k, the mapping $\mathbf{G}_k$ maps $\mathcal{L}(W)$ to

http://dx.doi.org/10.5772/intechopen.70420

$\mathcal{L}(V)$. It is also necessary to know the most represented coset $\mathbf{u} + W$ in $\mathcal{C}$. Using these notations, the cryptanalysis is formalized in Algorithm 3. Finally, to include potential information on the round keys, this attack processes only a subset $\mathcal{K}$ of $\mathscr{K}$.

```
Algorithm 3 - SelectKeys(G, G, K, C, u, V, NbCand)
Input. See Section 3.2.
Output. The set Cand containing the NbCand best keys together with their scores.

Cand ← []
For each k ∈ K do
    Computation of the score of k
    Score ← 0
    For each c ∈ C do
        t ← G(k, u)
        If G(k, c) lies in t + V then
            Score ← Score + 1
    Saving k if it is one of the NbCand best keys
    If the cardinality of Cand is lower than NbCand then
        Insert (k, Score) in Cand
        Else if Score is greater than the lowest score in Cand then
            Remove the lowest scored key of Cand
            Insert (k, Score) in Cand
    Return Cand
```

More generally, the parameters can be outlined as follows.

- The sets of all possible keys and ciphertexts are referred to as $\mathscr{K}$ and $\mathscr{C}$.
- The keyed mapping $G : \mathscr{K} \times \mathscr{C} \to E$ typically undoes (or partially undoes) one or two rounds of the encryption process.
- Its secret counterpart is denoted by $\mathbf{G} : \mathscr{K} \times \mathscr{C} \to E$. It is assumed that $\mathbf{G}_k$ maps a linear partition $\mathcal{L}(W)$ to another partition $\mathcal{L}(V)$ no matter the key k used.
- The set of the given ciphertexts is denoted by $\mathcal{C}$. The set of the keys that must be scored by this attack is denoted by $\mathcal{K}$.
- It is assumed that there is a coset of W containing significantly more ciphertexts than any other coset. The element $\mathbf{u}$ of $\mathscr{C}$ is a representative of this coset.
- Finally, `NbCand` is the number of candidate keys to return.

Remark 4.13. Taking a closer look at Algorithm 3, we can see that the structure `Cand` requires an efficient way to remove the lowest scored key. In our implementation, `Cand` is a sorted array of couples (s, L) where L is a list containing the keys having the score s. Since there are very few different scores, the sorted insertion in `Cand` is (almost) in constant time. Removing the lowest scored key is also in constant time. Thus, the time complexity of this cryptanalysis is $O(\#\mathcal{K} \times \#\mathcal{C})$.

4. Cryptanalysis of BEA-1 using the backdoor

The algorithm `SelectKeys` (see Algorithm 3) detailed into the previous section enables recovery of information on the last round key, using the fact that the round function acts as a function mapping a linear partition to another one with high probability. In this section, we explain how this algorithm can be used to recover the full 120-bit cipher key in just a few seconds on a laptop computer.

This cryptanalysis requires N = 2^{16} chosen plaintexts and their corresponding ciphertexts encrypted under one unknown cipher key K. As BEA-1 operates on 80-bit blocks, this amounts to 2×640 KiB of data. The plaintexts only need to be uniformly chosen in one coset of V, and there is no requirement on the cipher key.

Our cryptanalysis is naturally divided in five distinct parts. First, we give a brief overview of each part. By hypothesis, all the plaintexts are in the same coset of V. As explained in Section 2.1, a coset of W should be more represented among the ciphertexts. The first part is aimed at finding a representative $\mathbf{u}$ of this coset. The second part consists in using the algorithm `SelectKeys` to find 2^{15} candidates for the full 80-bit last round key $k^{[11]}$. Next, relying on a property of the key schedule, `SelectKeys` is applied to these 2^{15} candidates to find the right last key in a third part. So far, we have recovered 80 bits of the cipher key. Knowing the last round key, it is then possible to undo the last round of each ciphertext. The fourth part is really close to the first one and provides 2^{15} candidates for the 40 remaining bits. Finally, deduce the 2^{15} candidate cipher keys from $k^{[11]}$ and the preceding candidates. The last part involves testing these cipher keys on the plaintext/ciphertext pairs available to find the right one.

The presentation of our cryptanalysis is structured as follows. First, we provide the full attack in Algorithm 4. Then, each part of this algorithm is detailed in one dedicated section. It should be noted that we keep the notations of Section 2 (and not those of Section 3) in the remainder of this chapter. This work has been presented at the RusKrypto 2017 conference [31].

4.1. Part 1: finding the right output coset

Let $\mathcal{P}$ denote the set of the 2^{16} plaintexts uniformly chosen in one coset of V and let $\mathcal{C} = \{E_K(p) | p \in \mathcal{P}\}$ denote the set of their ciphertexts. As said previously, we first need to find the most represented coset of W in $\mathcal{C}$. Let U_i be the subspace of $\mathbb{F}_2^{10}$ defined by $U_i = L_{W_i}(\{*0\})$ for each $0 \leq i < 3$. Since $\{*0\}$ is a complement space of $\{0*\}$ and L_{W_i} is an automorphism, we know that U_i is a complement space of $L_{W_i}(\{0*\}) = W_i$. Define U as the subspace $\prod_{i=0}^{7} U_{i \bmod 4}$ of $(\mathbb{F}_2^{10})^8$. Of course, U is a complement space of W.

http://dx.doi.org/10.5772/intechopen.70420

Algorithm 4 - Cryptanalysis of BEA-1 Using the Backdoor

Input. The number N of plaintext/ciphertext pairs (typically, $\mathtt{N} \approx 2^{15}$).

- A set $\mathcal{P}$ of N plaintexts uniformly chosen in one coset of V.
- The corresponding ciphertexts encrypted under one (unknown) cipher key K. The set $\{E_K(p) \mid p \in \mathcal{P}\}$ of these ciphertexts in denoted by $\mathcal{C}$.

Output. The cipher key K or "Failure" in case of failure.

NbCand $\leftarrow 2^{15}$

Part 1: find the representative of the output coset.
    $\mathbf{u} \leftarrow$ the element $u \in U$ maximizing the cardinality of $\mathcal{C} \cap (u + W)$

Part 2: find the 2^{15} best candidates for $k^{[11]}$.
    $E \leftarrow \{3\}$
    Cand $\leftarrow \{(k_i)_{i \in E} \mid k_3 \in \mathbb{F}_2^{10}\}$
    For each idx $\in [7, 0, 4, 1, 5, 2, 6]$ **do**
        $E \leftarrow E \cup \{\mathtt{idx}\}$
        Define $\mathbf{G}_E$, G_E, $\mathcal{C}_E$ and V_E as in Section 4.2
        $\mathcal{K}_E \leftarrow \{(k_i)_{i \in E} \mid k_{\mathtt{idx}} \in \mathbb{F}_2^{10}$ and $(k_i)_{i \in E \setminus \{\mathtt{idx}\}} \in \mathtt{Cand}\}$
        Cand $\leftarrow$ SelectKeys$(\mathbf{G}_E, G_E, \mathcal{K}_E, \mathcal{C}_E, (\mathbf{u}_i)_{i \in E}, V_E, \mathtt{NbCand})$

Part 3: find $k^{[11]}$ among its candidates.
    $E \leftarrow \{0, 2, 5, 7\}$
    Define $\mathbf{G}$, G and V' as in Section 4.3
    Cand $\leftarrow$ SelectKeys$(\mathbf{G}, G, \mathtt{Cand}, \mathcal{C}_E, (\mathbf{u}_i)_{i \in E}, V, \mathtt{NbCand})$
    $k^{[11]} \leftarrow$ the key with the highest score in Cand

Part 4: find the 2^{15} best candidates for $({k'}_i^{[10]})_{4 \le i < 8}$.
    Define $\mathcal{C}'$ and $\mathbf{u}'$ as in Section 4.4
    $E \leftarrow \{4\}$
    Cand $\leftarrow \{(k'_i)_{i \in E} \mid k'_4 \in \mathbb{F}_2^{10}\}$
    For each idx $\in [7, 5, 6]$ **do**
        $E \leftarrow E \cup \{\mathtt{idx}\}$
        Define $\mathbf{G}_E$, G_E, $\mathcal{C}'_E$ and V_E as in Section 4.4
        $\mathcal{K}'_E \leftarrow \{(k'_i)_{i \in E} \mid k'_{\mathtt{idx}} \in \mathbb{F}_2^{10}$ and $(k'_i)_{i \in E \setminus \{\mathtt{idx}\}} \in \mathtt{Cand}\}$
        Cand $\leftarrow$ SelectKeys$(\mathbf{G}_E, G_E, \mathcal{K}'_E, \mathcal{C}'_E, (\mathbf{u}'_i)_{i \in E}, V_E, \mathtt{NbCand})$

Part 5: find the cipher key K.
    For each $({k'}_i^{[10]})_{4 \le i < 8} \in \mathtt{Cand}$ **do**
        $({k_i}^{[10]})_{4 \le i < 8} \leftarrow M(({k'}_i^{[10]})_{4 \le i < 8})$
        $K \leftarrow$ the cipher key corresponding to $({k_i}^{[10]})_{4 \le i < 8}$ and $k^{[11]}$
        If $E_K(p) = c$ for all plaintext/ciphertext pairs (p, c) **then**
            Return K
Return "Failure"

Let c be a ciphertext and $u = (u_i)_{i<8}$ be in U. Because both U and W are product spaces, it is easily seen that u is the unique representative in U of the coset $c + W$ if, and only if, c_i and u_i are in the same coset of $W_{i\text{mod}4}$ for each $i < 8$. We deduce the following efficient way to compute the representative in U of the coset $c + W$. First, precompute the four tables $\texttt{RepW}_i$ such that, for each x in $\mathbb{F}_2^{10}$, $\texttt{RepW}_i[x]$ gives the representative in U_i of $x + W_i$. These tables are just arrays of 1024 integers. Then, the representative of $c = (c_i)_{i<8}$ is just $u = (\texttt{RepW}_{i \bmod 4}[c_i])_{i<8}$.

To find the most represented coset of W in $\mathcal{C}$, we first compute the representative in U of each ciphertext as described above. Then, we search for the representative that occurs the most. Any naive algorithm should work since there are only 2^{15} representatives.

4.2. Part 2: obtaining candidates for the last round key

This part is intended to find candidates for the last round key $k^{[11]}$ using the algorithm SelectKeys (see Algorithm 3) to undo the last round of BEA-1. However, if this algorithm is naively applied, then the last round has to be undone for each of the 2^{16} ciphertexts and 2^{80} possible values of $k^{[11]}$, yielding an order of 2^{96} time complexity.

To solve this problem, the 2^{15} candidates for $k^{[11]}$ are obtained bundle by bundle, as illustrated in **Figure 4.8.** First, we partially decrypt the bundles of index 3 and 7. We begin by these

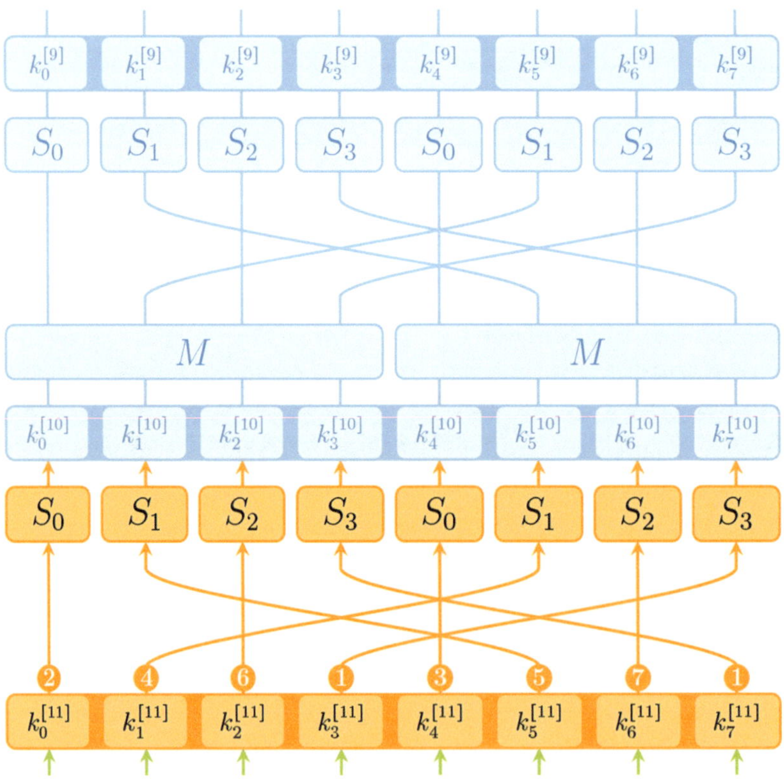

Figure 4.8. Cryptanalysis using the backdoor (Part 2).

bundles since they both involve the S-box S_3, being the most different from its secret equivalent. Following the notations of `SelectKeys`, the set containing the ciphertexts is $\mathcal{C}_{\{3,7\}} = \{(c_3, c_7) | c \in \mathcal{C}\}$, and the set of the keys is $\mathcal{K}_{\{3,7\}} = \{(k_3, k_7) | k_3, k_7 \in \mathbb{F}_2^{10}\}$. The mapping used to partially decrypt the last round of these ciphertexts is

$$G_{\{3,7\}} : (\mathbb{F}_2^{10})^2 \times (\mathbb{F}_2^{10})^2 \to (\mathbb{F}_2^{10})^2$$
$$((k_3, k_7), (c_3, c_7)) \mapsto (S_3^{-1}(c_3 + k_3), S_3^{-1}(c_7 + k_7)) .$$

Its secret equivalent $\mathbf{G}_{\{3,7\}}$ is obtained by replacing S_3 with $\mathbf{S}_3$. The two remaining inputs of the algorithm are the representative $\mathbf{u} = (\mathbf{u}_3, \mathbf{u}_7)$ of the most represented coset of $(W_3)^2$, and the subspace $(V_3)^2$ of $(\mathbb{F}_2^{10})^2$. It is worth observing that $\mathbf{G}_{\{3,7\}}$ maps $\mathcal{L}((W_3)^2)$ to $\mathcal{L}((V_3)^2)$ as required by the algorithm. Running `SelectKeys` with these arguments generates a set `Cand` containing 2^{15} candidates for $({k_3}^{[11]}, {k_7}^{[11]})$ instead of 2^{20}.

From now on, each step seeks to add a new bundle to our candidates for the last round key $k^{[11]}$. The next bundle to add has index 0. Let E denote the set {0, 3, 7} of the current bundle's indices. Since we have no information on the value of ${k_0}^{[11]}$, the set of the possible values for $({k_i}^{[11]})_{i \in E}$ is

$$\mathcal{K}_E = \{(k_i)_{i \in E} | k_0 \in \mathbb{F}_2^{10}, (k_3, k_7) \in \texttt{Cand}\} .$$

Following the idea of the first step, we define $\mathcal{C}_E = \{(c_i)_{i \in E} | (c_i)_{i<8} \in \mathcal{C}\}$ and

$$G_E : (\mathbb{F}_2^{10})^E \times (\mathbb{F}_2^{10})E \to (\mathbb{F}_2^{10})E$$
$$((k_i)_{i \in E}, (c_i)_{i \in E}) \mapsto (S_{i \bmod 4}^{-1}(c_i + k_i))i \in E \, .$$

Then, define $\mathbf{G}_E$ by replacing S_i with $\mathbf{S}_i$ and let V_E denote the subspace $\prod_{i \in E} V_{i \bmod 4}$ of $(\mathbb{F}_2^{10})^E$. The set `Cand` obtained by running `SelectKeys` with these parameters contains 2^{15} candidates for $({k_0}^{[11]}, {k_3}^{[11]}, {k_7}^{[11]})$.

According to Algorithm 4, the index of the next bundle is 4. Actually, the order of the bundle's indices was chosen such as to involve the S-boxes S_3, then S_0, S_1 and finally S_2. The current indices are in the set $E = \{0, 3, 4, 7\}$. Similarly, we define

$$\mathcal{K}_E = \{(k_i)_{i \in E} | k_4 \in \mathbb{F}_2^{10}, (k_0, k_3, k_7) \in \texttt{Cand}\}$$

to include the information on $k^{[11]}$ gathered by the previous step. Finally, define $\mathcal{C}_E$, G_E, $\mathbf{G}_E$ and V_E as above. Again, the algorithm `SelectKeys` yields 2^{15} candidates for $({k_i}^{[11]})_{i \in E}$.

This time, let us take a closer look at the implementation of this step. Because $\#\mathcal{K}_E = 2^{25}$ and $\#\mathcal{C}_E = 2^{16}$, a straightforward implementation of `SelectKeys` requires 2^{41} partial round decryptions, as explained by Remark 4.13. Algorithm 5 provides our implementation of `SelectKeys` for this step. As we can see, the previous candidates are used to filter the ciphertexts before attacking k_4 by brute force. For each of the 2^{15} candidates, initializing the filter requires 2^{16} partial decryptions. On average, it remains roughly 2^6 ciphertexts after the filtering process. The loop over k_4 hence requires 2^{16} partial decryptions. Consequently, this implementation performs about 2^{32} partial decryptions instead of 2^{41}.

Algorithm 5 - An implementation of the step idx=4 in part 2.

Cand ← []
For each of the 2^{15} candidates (k_0, k_3, k_7) for $(k_0^{[11]}, k_3^{[11]}, k_7^{[11]})$ **do**
    Initialization of the filter over the ciphertexts
    Filter $\leftarrow \varnothing$
    $(\mathbf{t}_0, \mathbf{t}_3, \mathbf{t}_7) \leftarrow (\mathbf{S}_0^{-1}(k_0 + \mathbf{u}_0), \mathbf{S}_3^{-1}(k_3 + \mathbf{u}_3), \mathbf{S}_3^{-1}(k_7 + \mathbf{u}_7))$
    For each $c \in \mathcal{C}$ **do**
        $(t_0, t_3, t_7) \leftarrow (S_0^{-1}(k_0 + c_0), S_3^{-1}(k_3 + c_3), S_3^{-1}(k_7 + c_7))$
        If $t_0 \in (\mathbf{t}_0 + V_0)$ and $t_3 \in (\mathbf{t}_3 + V_3)$ and $t_7 \in (\mathbf{t}_7 + V_3)$ **then**
            Filter ← Filter $\cup \{c\}$
    Loop over the new bundle of the key
    For each $k_4 \in \mathbb{F}_2^{10}$ **do**
        Score ← 0
        $\mathbf{t}_4 \leftarrow \mathbf{S}_0^{-1}(k_4 + \mathbf{u}_4)$
        For each $c \in$ Filter **do**
            $t_4 \leftarrow S_0^{-1}(k_4 + c_4)$
            If $t_4 \in (\mathbf{t}_4 + V_0)$ **then**
                Score ← Score + 1
        Saving (k_0, k_3, k_4, k_7) if its score is high enough
        If #Cand $\leq 2^{15}$ **then**
            Insert $((k_0, k_3, k_4, k_7)$, Score$)$ in Cand
            Else if Score is greater than the lowest score in Cand **then**
                Remove the lowest scored key of Cand
                Insert $((k_0, k_3, k_4, k_7)$, Score$)$ in Cand
Return Cand

Naturally, the 2^{15} candidates for the full round key $k^{[11]}$ are obtained by repeating this method for the four remaining bundles. We will conclude by observing that the complexity of each step decreases since the filtering process improves as the algorithm progresses.

4.3. Part 3: finding the last round key

So far, we have found 2^{15} candidates for the 80-bit key $k^{[11]}$. This part intends to recover the right key among these candidates, relying on the key schedule's structure. Let us consider the

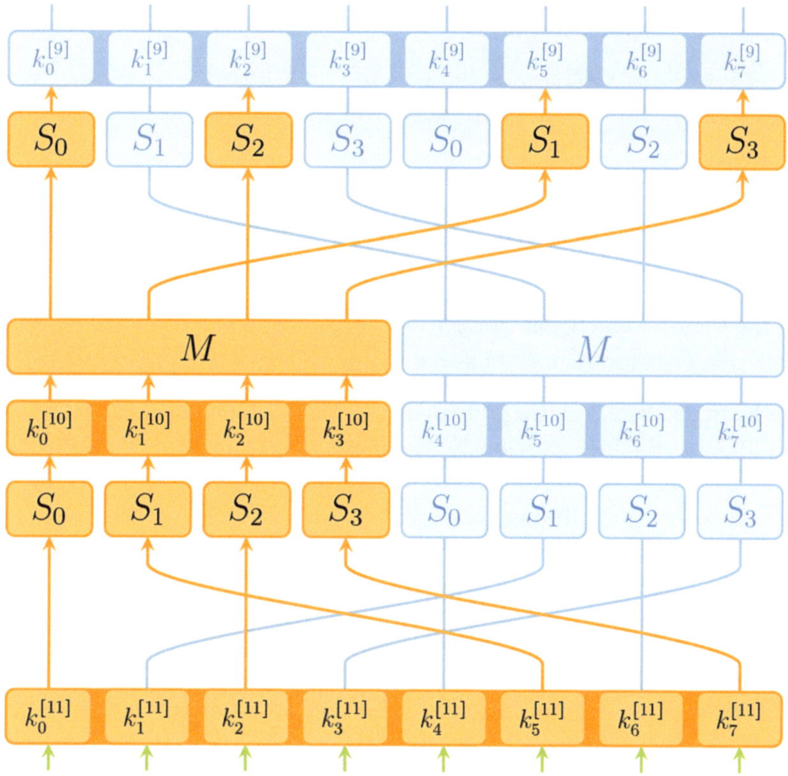

Figure 4.9. Cryptanalysis using the backdoor (Part 3).

last round of the key schedule in order to derive a relation between $k^{[10]}$ and $k^{[11]}$. In **Figure 4.2**:

- $k^{[9]} = (k_0{}^{[9]}, \ldots, k_7{}^{[9]})$ corresponds with $(k_0, \ldots, k_7)$,
- $k^{[10]} = (k_0{}^{[10]}, \ldots, k_7{}^{[10]})$ corresponds with $(k_8, \ldots, k_{15})$,
- $k^{[11]} = (k_0{}^{[11]}, \ldots, k_7{}^{[11]})$ corresponds with $(k_{16}, \ldots, k_{23})$.

It is then easily seen that

$$(k_0^{[10]}, k_1^{[10]}, k_2^{[10]}, k_3^{[10]}) = (k_0^{[11]}, k_1^{[11]}, k_2^{[11]}, k_3^{[11]}) + (k_4^{[11]}, k_5^{[11]}, k_6^{[11]}, k_7^{[11]}) .$$

Thus, the 40 leftmost bits of $k^{[10]}$ are determined by $k^{[11]}$. Using this equality, it is possible to partially decrypt the last two rounds for every candidate for $k^{[11]}$. Again, the algorithm `SelectKeys` is used to distinguish between candidates.

Instead of wasting time understanding the definition of G stated hereinafter, we encourage the reader to compare it with **Figure 4.9**, which speaks for itself. Let us consider

$$G' : (F_2^{10})^8 \times (\mathbb{F}_2^{10})\{0,2,5,7\} \mapsto (\mathbb{F}_2^{10})4$$
$$((k_i)_{i<8}, (c_i)_{i\in\{0,2,5,7\}}) \mapsto (S_0^{-1}(c_0+k_0)+k_0+k_4,\ S_1^{-1}(c_5+k_5)+k_1+k_5,$$
$$S_2^{-1}(c_2+k_2)+k_2+k_6,\ S_3^{-1}(c_7+k_7)+k_3+k_7)\,.$$

Then, let G be the mapping from $(F_2^{10})^8 \times (\mathbb{F}_2^{10})^{\{0,2,5,7\}}$ to $(\mathbb{F}_2^{10})^4$ given by

$$G = (S_0 \parallel S_1 \parallel S_2 \parallel S_3)^{-1} \circ M^{-1} \circ G'\,.$$

Define **G** in the same way as before and let $V' = \prod_{i=0}^{3} V_i$. Finally, run `Selectkeys` as in line 12 of Algorithm 4. The candidate that has the highest score is then the last round key $k^{[11]}$.

To explain why Parts 2 and 3 of this cryptanalysis are complementary, let us take a closer look at the 2^{15} candidates obtained previously. Most of them are in fact really close to $k^{[11]}$; more precisely, they have at most three bundles different from $k^{[11]}$. This observation is not surprising because when decrypting the last round, each bundle of the key affects only one bundle of the output. As a direct consequence, close candidates give rise to close one-round decrypted ciphertexts. This explains why the algorithm `SelectKeys`, as used in Part 2, may assign similar scores to close candidates.

By contrast, the mapping G defined above yields very different outputs when used with close candidate keys. Such a property comes from the high diffusion provided by M^{-1}. Thus, this part is more effective where the previous part has its main weakness. Moreover, the side effects are limited here since we decrypt two rounds instead of one.

4.4. Part 4: obtaining candidates for the remaining bits

The round function of the key schedule being bijective, it is sufficient to know the 120 output bits of the last round to compute the cipher key. Until now, we have recovered the last round key $k^{[11]}$, accounting for 80 of these 120 bits. The 40 remaining bits are the 40 rightmost bits of $k^{[10]}$, also denoted by $(k_i^{[10]})_{4\le i<8}$. This fourth part intends to find 2^{15} candidates for these unknown bits.

Since the key $k^{[11]}$ is now known, it is possible to undo the last round for every ciphertext. The cryptanalysis is then reduced to the attack of the second to last round. However, the method used in Part 2 cannot be directly applied here since the second to last round involves the MDS mapping M. Let x and k be elements of $(\mathbb{F}_2^{10})^4$ and observe that

$$M(x)+k = M(x)+M(M^{-1}(k)) = M(x+M^{-1}(k)) = M(x+k')$$

where $k' = M^{-1}(k)$. Thus, the key addition and the mapping M can be switched provided that the key is replaced. According to this observation, define

$$(k_{i'}^{[10]})_{4\le i<8} = M^{-1}((k_i^{[10]})_{4\le i<8})\,.$$

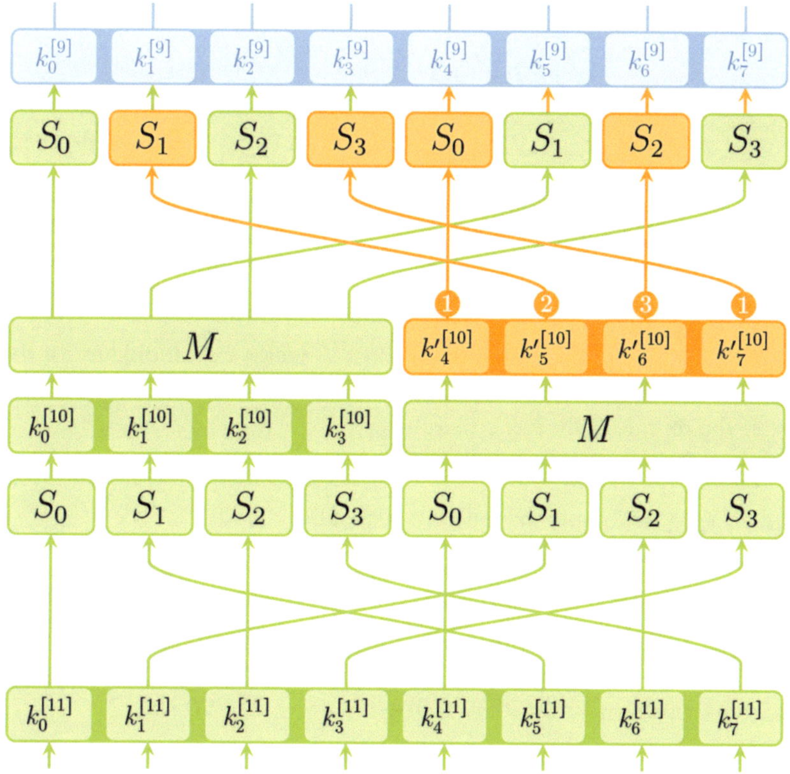

Figure 4.10. Cryptanalysis using the backdoor (Part 4).

Therefore, the last two rounds of BEA-1 can equivalently be represented as in **Figure 4.10.**

Thanks to this representation, candidates for the key $(k'^{[10]}_i)_{4 \le i < 8}$ can be obtained using `SelectKeys` as in Part 2. To this end, we first need to partially undo the last round using $k^{[11]}$. Following **Figure 4.10**, define

$$\begin{aligned} f : (\mathbb{F}_2^{10})^{\{1,3,4,6\}} &\rightarrow (\mathbb{F}_2^{10})_4 \\ (c_i)i \in \{1,3,4,6\} &\mapsto M^{-1}(S_0^{-1}(c_4 + k_4{}^{[11]}), S_1^{-1}(c_1 + k_1{}^{[11]}), \\ &\qquad S_2^{-1}(c_6 + k_6{}^{[11]}), S_3^{-1}(c_3 + k_3{}^{[11]}))\,. \end{aligned}$$

The set $\{f((c_i)_{i \in \{1,3,4,6\}}) | c \in \mathcal{C}\}$ of these "new" ciphertexts is denoted by $\mathcal{C}'$, and the corresponding coset representative is $\mathbf{u}' = \mathbf{f}((\mathbf{u}_i)_{i \in \{1,3,4,6\}})$. To be more consistent with **Figure 4.10**, the bundles of $\mathbf{u}'$ and of the elements of $\mathcal{C}'$ are indexed from 4 to 7 included. The remainder of the attack is similar to Part 2 as the candidates are obtained bundle by bundle. The first step gets candidates for the bundle's indices 4 and 7. The second and the third steps add the indices 5 and 6, respectively. If E denotes the set of the current bundle's indices, then the parameters of `SelectKeys` are the set $\mathcal{C}'_E = \{(c'_i)_{i \in E} | (c'_i)_{4 \le i < 8} \in \mathcal{C}'\}$, the mapping

$$G_E : (\mathbb{F}_2^{10})^E \times (\mathbb{F}_2^{10})E \to (\mathbb{F}_2^{10})^E$$
$$((k'_i)_{i\in E'}(c'_i)_{i\in E}) \mapsto (S^{-1}_{i \bmod 4}(c'_i + k'_i))_{i\in E},$$

its equivalent $\mathbf{G}_E$ and the subspace $V_E = \prod_{i\in E} V_{i \bmod 4}$ of $(\mathbb{F}_2^{10})^E$. The other details are given in Algorithm 4. At the end of this part, every candidate $k' = (k'_i)_{4\leq i<8}$ for $(k'_i{}^{[10]})_{4\leq i<8}$ gives rise to a candidate $k = M(k')$ for $(k_i^{[10]})_{4\leq i<8}$.

4.5. Part 5: deducing the cipher key

Concatenating the candidates for $(k_i^{[10]})_{4\leq i<8}$ with $k^{[11]}$ yields 2^{15} candidates for the output of the key schedule's last round. To obtain the corresponding candidates for the cipher key, we need to reverse the rounds of the key schedule.

Referring to **Figure 4.2**, the ith round of the key schedule maps the element (X_0, X_1, X_2) of $(\mathbb{F}_2^{40})^3$ to (Y_0, Y_1, Y_2) according to the following equalities

$$Y_0 = X_0 + f_i(X_2), \quad Y_1 = Y_0 + X_1, \quad Y_2 = Y_1 + X_2,$$

where f_i denotes the permutation of $(\mathbb{F}_2^{10})^4$ defined for each X by

$$f_i(X) = (3^i \bmod 2^{10}, 0, 0, 0) + (S_0 \parallel S_1 \parallel S_2 \parallel S_3) \circ M(X).$$

Using these notations, it easily seen that

$$X_0 = Y_0 + f_i(Y_1 + Y_2), \quad X_1 = Y_0 + Y_1, \quad X_2 = Y_1 + Y_2.$$

These equalities describe how to reverse each round of the key schedule, and thus how to recover the 2^{15} candidate cipher keys.

Finally, it just remains to test these candidate cipher keys to complete the cryptanalysis. To be efficient, choose one plaintext/ciphertext pair (p, c) and check whether or not the encryption of p under the candidate K is equal to c. In case of equality, repeat this process for all pairs available to prevent false positive results. Otherwise, the candidate is discarded. Obviously, the right cipher key is the one that passes all tests.

http://dx.doi.org/10.5772/intechopen.70420

Conclusion

In this book, we have addressed the following issue: "is it possible to design a mathematical backdoor which would rely mostly on suitable partitionning techniques of the plaintext and ciphertext spaces, independently of the round keys?". We had in mind initially to exploit combinatorial properties of the core primitives.

The overall conclusion we get is that if we want to design such a backdoor, the only solution is to stay in the algebraic domain and no specifically combinatorial tools or primitive are possible. Let us summarize in details the main results.

If we wish to design any encryption system that maps any partition $\mathcal{A}$ of the plaintexts to a partition $\mathcal{B}$ of the ciphertexts, independently of the round keys then

- the round function must map a linear partition to another one, and
- at least one S-box must do the same.

Here, the backdoor is precisely the knowledge of the pair $(\mathcal{A}, \mathcal{B})$. This result implies that the partitions considered for the backdoor belong to the algebraic domain and not to the combinatorial one. We are condemned to consider highly structured algebraic objects.

For the candidate S-boxes which make it possible to design such a backdoor, we have performed a detailed study with respect to their linear and differential tables. We have given lower bounds on their linear and differential uniformities and we have explained how to (nearly) achieve them.

The study presented in this book shows that the linear and differential tables of these backdoor S-boxes are highly structured. Thus, we have proved that our backdoor class implies necessarily a high algebraic structure. We conjecture that the reverse may be also true: *any algebraic structure can be used to design a backdoor cipher*. In terms of backdoor detectability, we also surmise that *it is easy to detect and identify our backdoor from the results presented in this book*.

As future works, we would primarily address the two following issues. First, what would the results be if we consider dependent round keys? In other words, we would like to consider a key schedule algorithm which therefore would be part of the backdoor.

Second, we want to explore and formalize exhaustively a criterion which would help either to design better hidden backdoors or, on the contrary, to evaluate the presence of a potential backdoor. The first idea of criterion is the following. Let $\mathcal{S}$ denote the set of the S-boxes mapping a linear partition to another linear partition. For any S-box S we define the distance with respect to $\mathcal{S}$ as follows

$$\min\{\#\,\mathrm{Supp}\,(\tau) | \tau \in \mathfrak{S}(\mathbb{F}_2^n), S \circ \tau \in \mathcal{S}\}\,.$$

This represents the minimal number of images under S we have to modify in order to obtain an S-box lying in $\mathcal{S}$. In other words, the aim is to have a distance measure to a backdoor S-box. In Chapter 4, Section 2, we have first considered secret S-boxes mapping linear partitions to another ones. Unfortunately, as mentioned previously, the structure of their linear and differential tables is likely to betray the existence of a backdoor and can be used to find it. This is the reason why, we have then modified the S-boxes. These new S-boxes "behave" similarly to their secret counterparts with high probability. We have published a first-algorithm proposal [32] denoted BEA-1 (*Backdoored Encryption Algorithm version 1*) whose backdoor is based on this property. It operates on 80-bit data blocks using a 120-bit cipher key and is directly inspired by the AES. The knowledge of the backdoor enables recovery of the full cipher key in just a few seconds on a laptop computer using only 2^{16} chosen plaintext blocks.

We also hope to develop our work further to explore the different classes of possible backdoors. In order to have a clearer view of the research presented in this book, we outline a tentative starting classification of backdoor techniques. Of course, we hope that other authors will have a critical cross-view of it and will make it evolve.

- *Backdoors based on a single mathematical weakness*. The backdoor is essentially put in the core cryptographic primitives, exploits algebraic or combinatorial properties and is independent of the key and the plaintext.
- *Backdoors based on the combination of mixed techniques*. Here, the backdoor relies on the combination of several factors: algebraic properties, combinatorial properties, environmental use of the algorithm (for example the nature of the plaintext encoding). Each aspects being taken separately, it is not possible to see the backdoor. Only the combined and global view makes it possible to see it, possibly. This approach seems promising in the light our study of real-life governmental encryption algorithms proposed in a more or less recent past.

Laval, France

May 26th, 2017

Appendix

See **Figures 1A** to **11A**.

x	200	100	080	040	020	010	008	004	002	001
$L_{V_0}(x)$	334	259	21D	0E4	193	266	343	3ED	354	17F
$L_{V_1}(x)$	3DA	306	39E	262	080	398	229	34C	251	37B
$L_{V_2}(x)$	295	237	131	3D1	26B	0BA	155	307	37E	318
$L_{V_3}(x)$	290	15D	0F8	2BE	25F	1D1	21E	134	0DC	15A
$L_{W_0}(x)$	3E8	386	067	19C	158	16A	11B	306	05E	0B8
$L_{W_1}(x)$	364	33E	3A7	119	1D2	04B	3B7	0D5	027	2C8
$L_{W_2}(x)$	324	188	3CB	1B0	131	1A9	095	107	36F	2A3
$L_{W_3}(x)$	262	1A5	34E	0B7	3ED	0F0	2FE	191	332	1A6
$(L_{V_0})^{-1}(x)$	3BF	268	0BB	379	17B	055	061	2F9	354	1F2
$(L_{V_1})^{-1}(x)$	13D	0AD	020	2C7	36D	2B4	314	047	0D7	14C
$(L_{V_2})^{-1}(x)$	361	070	133	02A	2B8	3CC	0DC	21A	08B	184
$(L_{V_3})^{-1}(x)$	1E9	3D1	0BE	245	0F6	357	1DA	074	318	26D
$(L_{W_0})^{-1}(x)$	026	0E9	104	29D	351	053	207	3F9	332	187
$(L_{W_1})^{-1}(x)$	142	1B0	070	3D3	196	088	2E0	0B7	2BB	398
$(L_{W_2})^{-1}(x)$	02D	0AA	205	0F1	375	19A	3AF	1F2	339	265
$(L_{W_3})^{-1}(x)$	0A6	3B3	045	32B	1E4	29A	2AD	27A	069	168

Figure 1A. The transformation mappings given over the standard basis of $\mathbb{F}_2^{10}$.

x	$x \times M_U$	$x \times M_V$	$P_{U\to V}(x)$
(10, 00, 00, 00)	(07, 06, 1E, 17)	(0E, 16, 02, 14)	(07, 01, 1C, 18)
(08, 00, 00, 00)	(11, 03, 0F, 19)	(07, 0B, 01, 0A)	(05, 16, 14, 03)
(04, 00, 00, 00)	(1A, 13, 15, 1E)	(11, 17, 12, 05)	(0A, 01, 1C, 1C)
(02, 00, 00, 00)	(0D, 1B, 18, 0F)	(1A, 19, 09, 10)	(02, 1F, 1E, 1C)
(01, 00, 00, 00)	(14, 1F, 0C, 15)	(0D, 1E, 16, 08)	(01, 1B, 13, 04)
(00, 10, 00, 00)	(06, 07, 17, 1E)	(16, 0E, 14, 02)	(07, 08, 01, 11)
(00, 08, 00, 00)	(03, 11, 19, 0F)	(0B, 07, 0A, 01)	(02, 1E, 1B, 1F)
(00, 04, 00, 00)	(13, 1A, 1E, 15)	(17, 11, 05, 12)	(16, 06, 1E, 0D)
(00, 02, 00, 00)	(1B, 0D, 0F, 18)	(19, 1A, 10, 09)	(0F, 11, 0C, 16)
(00, 01, 00, 00)	(1F, 14, 15, 0C)	(1E, 0D, 08, 16)	(11, 0E, 02, 0A)
(00, 00, 10, 00)	(1E, 17, 07, 06)	(02, 14, 0E, 16)	(1F, 0C, 08, 1B)
(00, 00, 08, 00)	(0F, 19, 11, 03)	(01, 0A, 07, 0B)	(17, 15, 17, 16)
(00, 00, 04, 00)	(15, 1E, 1A, 13)	(12, 05, 11, 17)	(1D, 04, 0E, 00)
(00, 00, 02, 00)	(18, 0F, 0D, 1B)	(09, 10, 1A, 19)	(11, 0E, 19, 15)
(00, 00, 01, 00)	(0C, 15, 14, 1F)	(16, 08, 0D, 1E)	(16, 1F, 06, 14)
(00, 00, 00, 10)	(17, 1E, 06, 07)	(14, 02, 16, 0E)	(0F, 03, 16, 03)
(00, 00, 00, 08)	(19, 0F, 03, 11)	(0A, 01, 0B, 07)	(0B, 12, 03, 0D)
(00, 00, 00, 04)	(1E, 15, 13, 1A)	(05, 12, 17, 11)	(1F, 1D, 1B, 02)
(00, 00, 00, 02)	(0F, 18, 1B, 0D)	(10, 09, 19, 1A)	(18, 12, 0A, 15)
(00, 00, 00, 01)	(15, 0C, 1F, 14)	(08, 16, 1E, 0D)	(17, 05, 05, 05)

Figure 2A. The linear mappings over $(\mathbb{F}_2^{10})^4$ associated to M_U, M_V and the linear mapping $P_{U\to V}$.

x	$M(x)$	$M^{-1}(x)$
(200, 000, 000, 000)	(13E, 20F, 253, 0BC)	(2D8, 209, 353, 243)
(100, 000, 000, 000)	(35C, 13E, 212, 110)	(0F5, 1BD, 210, 210)
(080, 000, 000, 000)	(32C, 199, 2C5, 07A)	(1E9, 3FE, 238, 329)
(040, 000, 000, 000)	(3C6, 010, 0EC, 261)	(002, 246, 2E2, 380)
(020, 000, 000, 000)	(231, 120, 322, 016)	(322, 3FD, 3D5, 0E5)
(010, 000, 000, 000)	(2D9, 10A, 0C4, 095)	(0AD, 337, 3C5, 2D4)
(008, 000, 000, 000)	(215, 11F, 1E0, 2E7)	(08D, 04D, 016, 34C)
(004, 000, 000, 000)	(23F, 15B, 0C7, 0A7)	(1AB, 11E, 05F, 3A4)
(002, 000, 000, 000)	(344, 394, 342, 165)	(1AE, 1E9, 2CB, 245)
(001, 000, 000, 000)	(112, 1BC, 36C, 0C5)	(10B, 221, 09D, 398)
(000, 200, 000, 000)	(0E6, 0ED, 314, 289)	(395, 295, 38D, 129)
(000, 100, 000, 000)	(17E, 011, 198, 3C5)	(2D7, 1F4, 378, 157)
(000, 080, 000, 000)	(15E, 0BF, 1E2, 04F)	(0BD, 1B1, 18E, 2AB)
(000, 040, 000, 000)	(006, 131, 32E, 12B)	(3AA, 29E, 239, 1C0)
(000, 020, 000, 000)	(39A, 062, 38C, 2EB)	(3D9, 069, 21B, 11B)
(000, 010, 000, 000)	(1F4, 1C5, 1FF, 31D)	(06D, 1BE, 3EB, 0BE)
(000, 008, 000, 000)	(022, 37D, 08D, 3D4)	(3D1, 236, 09D, 2F1)
(000, 004, 000, 000)	(13B, 2FA, 328, 38C)	(0EB, 2FD, 3C3, 176)
(000, 002, 000, 000)	(0CC, 32A, 01A, 2DB)	(055, 128, 25A, 17F)
(000, 001, 000, 000)	(237, 252, 004, 0F8)	(07D, 2BB, 037, 3C8)
(000, 000, 200, 000)	(009, 175, 254, 3ED)	(0A6, 050, 36D, 016)
(000, 000, 100, 000)	(2D5, 29F, 072, 04D)	(263, 36C, 361, 369)
(000, 000, 080, 000)	(09A, 1DD, 336, 34B)	(0C8, 111, 34B, 38E)
(000, 000, 040, 000)	(269, 2CC, 27E, 1CD)	(169, 1A1, 02D, 39B)
(000, 000, 020, 000)	(1B2, 0A7, 178, 208)	(009, 1D9, 3CC, 131)
(000, 000, 010, 000)	(189, 2AB, 1A6, 39D)	(141, 222, 031, 28A)
(000, 000, 008, 000)	(0DC, 0B1, 061, 3DE)	(1C7, 3F1, 063, 33C)
(000, 000, 004, 000)	(019, 08E, 280, 1A7)	(084, 128, 167, 20B)
(000, 000, 002, 000)	(38B, 1A6, 221, 260)	(0D0, 34D, 18C, 354)
(000, 000, 001, 000)	(075, 380, 371, 2E9)	(15E, 23B, 378, 376)
(000, 000, 000, 200)	(099, 176, 3BC, 031)	(03D, 208, 27E, 249)
(000, 000, 000, 100)	(38E, 3D2, 2CD, 21C)	(005, 38F, 215, 2DF)
(000, 000, 000, 080)	(1C7, 259, 17E, 0BE)	(14F, 3D2, 0E2, 1C7)
(000, 000, 000, 040)	(165, 3BA, 19B, 0F7)	(211, 2D9, 1B2, 362)
(000, 000, 000, 020)	(37F, 282, 3A4, 3D8)	(13C, 355, 058, 07F)
(000, 000, 000, 010)	(256, 130, 382, 067)	(19A, 0E6, 364, 0F2)
(000, 000, 000, 008)	(370, 1D0, 3CD, 07F)	(322, 319, 244, 300)
(000, 000, 000, 004)	(22D, 1C8, 221, 18B)	(2BE, 1DD, 223, 1FA)
(000, 000, 000, 002)	(058, 044, 3A0, 281)	(04A, 1EC, 1B6, 3B4)
(000, 000, 000, 001)	(28D, 172, 3EA, 24E)	(015, 371, 2DC, 0E2)

Figure 3A. Specification of the diffusion M and its inverse M^{-1}.

	..0	..1	..2	..3	..4	..5	..6	..7	..8	..9	..A	..B	..C	..D	..E	..F
00.	0BA	026	0A0	1E1	183	3DB	1A4	084	110	350	085	2E5	3B4	195	359	2E6
01.	33A	26B	209	07E	1CE	2E3	0C0	136	129	0C8	3D6	054	040	3F2	09F	322
02.	11B	07F	139	07D	2CF	02A	268	227	10A	1C5	12B	016	16C	20D	1E7	35B
03.	313	0CD	11E	1E6	117	355	182	0E6	094	1B9	19C	28C	255	336	0AF	19D
04.	2BC	1A9	31B	02E	282	2AE	272	2E9	3AA	1DD	013	2D3	30F	35A	159	1BB
05.	3DD	12A	248	3C7	28B	191	025	173	018	38D	1A1	185	007	156	378	312
06.	10B	143	05D	3FA	038	3DE	081	0F9	2D1	3FB	1C7	302	1DC	16A	2D8	23F
07.	030	1EB	3AF	311	36D	3BD	3C9	348	261	1AF	071	3EE	3BA	3AB	1B8	3CA
08.	290	118	21B	0F6	3FF	122	1B2	360	1D6	1B6	3D4	3BB	3B3	0EA	097	308
09.	3A9	086	0AE	15A	253	058	0BB	3D5	14B	1A3	23E	053	35D	277	384	0E2
0A.	233	2B8	2AF	0D0	1B1	105	0B3	215	2A2	27F	2DB	17E	12C	3A2	18E	2AC
0B.	321	09C	294	04C	036	2F1	3D2	18D	14C	304	128	069	198	2F4	3DC	370
0C.	138	324	23C	1FD	082	247	005	0A3	0F0	273	152	17B	1A0	1C8	04E	132
0D.	12F	0CC	075	10E	3E0	021	1AE	211	3E6	17A	276	289	0A9	123	01F	048
0E.	201	08F	0B1	002	179	32E	120	1AC	1E3	109	079	37C	297	096	12D	323
0F.	165	0AC	18B	0AB	1FF	13D	25B	3D3	111	22B	21C	1BE	187	30E	34A	318
10.	269	343	29F	395	1AD	1D2	023	3ED	1B3	35E	2D7	044	0F1	3F1	310	0A7
11.	287	3C3	2A5	213	3E4	3DA	0FD	140	38E	2C2	154	254	15F	02C	1FB	1ED
12.	1C6	051	062	090	214	230	190	15D	0A1	186	032	0B9	1DA	239	3D1	383
13.	331	06D	02D	009	2FC	3AD	2AA	363	1EF	38F	39A	2DC	3BF	106	39B	31F
14.	03E	0DE	1BC	067	0CF	155	2CE	240	05E	0E8	0C4	149	08C	3E5	2A1	150
15.	1D1	228	3DF	0E0	3F6	193	19B	27D	2B0	35C	0E3	171	180	022	00E	358
16.	161	0EE	365	15B	0C3	2CD	3E1	06C	119	283	31E	2B9	212	226	076	382
17.	38C	1D3	15C	0B2	22C	314	056	216	364	11C	1E9	020	176	389	2F2	073
18.	06F	27E	027	14E	177	26D	1BA	0EC	033	194	3C6	2F9	221	0E1	3F4	0B7
19.	14F	293	144	0FB	2F0	2F3	0F4	1CC	0C6	065	028	315	3E2	2DD	274	0FA
1A.	17C	041	080	2C5	072	08D	339	2A3	1F1	1DF	2F5	28A	015	188	246	206
1B.	091	03F	259	18F	1C3	27B	319	153	0D2	0BD	2D0	064	000	379	2F6	2A9
1C.	142	0F5	3EF	03B	3F8	344	3BC	265	0E7	334	238	08E	0AA	174	267	162
1D.	112	1D0	01C	292	2C0	0E9	2B6	301	0C1	30D	369	1C0	1E4	1F7	08A	2FA
1E.	3CB	34D	2BE	28F	09A	39D	232	262	333	2F8	397	2C4	06E	27A	317	017
1F.	327	26C	325	167	05B	36C	362	004	3F7	0F7	20B	22D	222	2D2	0CA	196
20.	33F	347	17D	349	146	170	367	18A	1DE	0B5	099	3BE	2C1	0BC	2A0	01B
21.	11D	010	342	169	366	2EC	088	361	291	131	2FF	199	18C	3B0	00D	24F
22.	031	063	3B6	281	0A5	070	1CB	07B	270	2CC	398	32B	1C1	396	278	39E
23.	160	0FF	1A2	0D4	024	24B	178	1BD	326	2EF	28D	299	21F	24A	103	042
24.	141	256	229	218	0EB	260	145	050	035	0E5	300	3AE	1E2	34E	223	20A
25.	164	02F	0C5	210	1A6	258	3F5	32D	1B4	2EA	1C4	3D0	381	371	392	101
26.	3C8	3F3	1F2	10F	0D1	1BF	2D6	320	390	25E	249	341	33B	203	3B5	23A
27.	09E	095	2C8	3A6	0F2	263	108	3B9	3E8	3C4	2BB	2B7	36E	13E	2C9	376
28.	014	00F	0DA	133	163	05C	0A4	1E5	019	37D	043	1FC	184	07A	3FE	03D
29.	0FE	25F	26E	3B7	21A	2E8	3B1	1B7	012	2CA	0C2	113	001	271	1D8	275
2A.	16F	1C9	0AD	236	2AB	3CF	3EC	24E	3F0	1D4	3CC	2BF	2C3	338	1B5	25C
2B.	181	052	243	1F3	11F	2EE	332	32C	1CD	3A8	2B4	34F	0D3	305	006	124
2C.	13F	13C	19E	3A0	2DE	2E2	3CE	345	3CD	0EF	205	31A	23D	34C	059	19F
2D.	1E0	307	3F9	217	337	0DB	14D	353	127	0CE	385	114	107	3D7	057	288
2E.	04F	2B2	2CB	039	234	2B5	2E1	32A	2FB	115	116	37B	3A5	092	373	17F
2F.	21E	06B	087	2FD	2ED	2BA	1EA	125	208	16E	2FE	2E0	0B4	3C2	3C1	21D
30.	11A	01D	3EA	047	157	25D	1D9	37F	16D	20E	098	2B1	340	22E	241	078
31.	1F5	0ED	192	298	3A7	30C	1CF	05F	351	0E4	335	046	151	24C	1EE	235
32.	12E	2A6	1A5	061	3A1	29C	011	066	093	03A	38A	1F8	1F0	3B2	134	356
33.	225	20C	3D9	2E4	0A8	0BE	1FE	0FC	0C7	377	2F7	07C	074	045	1E8	05A
34.	36B	36F	37E	375	04D	1FA	257	13B	089	220	399	00B	158	2D5	068	280
35.	357	0DD	0BF	1B0	2A7	23B	1CA	3FC	00A	330	2A4	200	3EB	008	126	0A6
36.	09B	37A	284	2D4	0F3	28E	237	31D	0DF	368	386	060	374	31C	29A	26A
37.	100	394	1F9	04B	391	39F	30B	00C	077	2EB	01A	231	29B	049	202	224
38.	0C9	2DA	2A8	286	06A	189	130	279	1EC	29D	104	387	32F	316	207	137
39.	0DC	02B	1D7	034	354	39C	0B6	329	3E3	3A4	0D9	245	2B3	0D6	33E	252
3A.	0CB	1DB	172	296	14A	04A	244	250	1F6	2AD	2C6	346	09D	388	328	3A3
3B.	2C7	3E7	29E	3C0	0D5	22A	1F4	168	3FD	242	102	3C5	0F8	251	264	2DF
3C.	27C	029	003	38B	10C	380	10D	295	303	197	33C	219	13A	306	166	2D9
3D.	175	19A	0D8	3D8	0A2	26F	3B8	1C2	148	30A	0B8	24D	1A7	121	15E	372
3E.	25A	266	22F	135	0B0	055	01E	3AC	083	285	34B	1D5	3E9	393	2E7	037
3F.	20F	0D7	1A8	1AB	16B	36A	352	204	2BD	08B	147	1AA	35F	03C	309	33D

Figure 4A. Specification of the secret S-box $\mathbf{S}_0$.

	..0	..1	..2	..3	..4	..5	..6	..7	..8	..9	..A	..B	..C	..D	..E	..F
00.	0BA	026	0A0	1E1	183	3DB	1A4	083	110	350	085	2E5	3B4	195	359	2E6
01.	33A	26B	209	217	1CE	2E3	0C0	136	129	0C8	3D6	054	040	3F2	09F	322
02.	11B	07F	139	07D	2CF	02A	268	227	246	1C5	12B	3B6	16C	20D	1E7	35B
03.	313	0CD	11E	1E6	117	355	182	0E6	094	1B9	19C	28C	2B9	336	0AF	19D
04.	2BC	1A9	31B	02E	282	2AE	272	2E9	3AA	1DD	013	2D3	30F	35A	159	1BB
05.	11C	12A	248	3C7	28B	191	025	173	018	38D	1A1	185	007	156	378	312
06.	0C9	143	05D	3FA	038	3DE	081	0F9	2D1	3FB	1C7	3E0	1DC	16A	2D8	23F
07.	030	1EB	3AF	311	36D	3BD	3C9	348	261	1AF	071	3EE	3BA	3AB	1B8	3CA
08.	22B	118	279	0F6	3FF	122	1B2	360	1D6	1B6	3D4	3BB	3B3	0EA	097	308
09.	3A9	086	0AE	15A	253	058	0BB	3D5	01D	1A3	23E	053	35D	277	384	0E2
0A.	233	2B8	2AF	0D0	1B1	105	0B3	215	2A2	27F	2DB	17E	12C	3A2	18E	2AC
0B.	321	09C	294	04C	036	2F1	3D2	18D	188	349	128	069	198	2F4	3DC	370
0C.	138	324	23C	1FD	082	247	005	0A3	0F0	273	152	17B	1A0	1C8	04E	34C
0D.	12F	0CC	075	10E	290	021	1AE	211	3E6	17A	276	289	3B5	123	01F	048
0E.	201	08F	29A	002	179	32E	120	1AC	1E3	109	079	37C	297	096	12D	323
0F.	165	0AC	18B	0AB	1FF	230	25B	3D3	111	07E	21C	1BE	187	30E	34A	318
10.	269	343	29F	395	1AD	1D2	023	2DE	1B3	35E	2D7	044	206	3F1	310	0A7
11.	287	3C3	2A5	213	3E4	3DA	0FD	140	38E	2C2	154	254	15F	02C	1FB	1ED
12.	1C6	051	062	090	214	14B	190	15D	0A1	186	032	0B9	1DA	239	3D1	383
13.	331	06D	02D	009	2FC	3AD	2AA	363	1EF	38F	39A	2DC	3BF	106	39B	31F
14.	03E	0DE	1BC	067	0CF	155	2CE	240	05E	0E8	0C4	149	08C	3E5	2A1	150
15.	1D1	228	3DF	0E0	3F6	193	19B	27D	2B0	35C	0E3	171	180	022	00E	358
16.	161	0EE	365	15B	0C3	2CD	3E1	06C	119	283	0F1	3B9	212	226	076	382
17.	38C	1D3	15C	0B2	22C	314	056	216	364	3DD	1E9	020	176	389	2F2	073
18.	06F	27E	027	14E	177	26D	1BA	0EC	25A	194	3C6	2F9	221	0E1	3F4	0B7
19.	14F	293	144	0FB	2F0	3ED	0F4	1CC	0C6	065	028	315	3E2	2DD	274	0FA
1A.	0D3	041	080	2C5	072	08D	339	2A3	1F1	1DF	2F5	267	015	0B1	275	21B
1B.	091	03F	259	18F	1C3	27B	319	153	0D2	0BD	2D0	064	000	379	2F6	2A9
1C.	142	0F5	3EF	03B	3F8	344	3BC	265	0E7	334	238	08E	347	174	18C	162
1D.	112	1D0	01C	292	2C0	0E9	2B6	301	0C1	30D	369	1C0	1E4	1F7	08A	2FA
1E.	3CB	34D	2BE	28F	09A	39D	232	262	333	2F8	397	2C4	06E	27A	317	017
1F.	327	26C	325	167	05B	36C	362	004	3F7	0F7	20B	22D	222	2D2	0CA	196
20.	33F	3B2	17D	302	146	170	367	18A	1DE	0B5	099	3BE	2C1	0BC	2A0	01B
21.	11D	010	342	169	366	2EC	088	361	291	131	2FF	199	1CA	3B0	00D	24F
22.	2B7	063	3EB	281	0A5	070	1CB	07B	270	2CC	398	32B	1C1	396	278	39E
23.	160	0FF	1A2	0D4	024	24B	178	1BD	326	2EF	28D	392	21F	24A	10B	042
24.	141	256	229	218	0EB	260	145	050	035	0E5	300	3AE	1E2	34E	223	20A
25.	164	02F	0C5	210	1A6	258	3F5	32D	1B4	2EA	1C4	3D0	381	371	2D9	101
26.	3C8	3F3	1F2	10F	0D1	1BF	2D6	320	390	25E	249	341	33B	203	087	23A
27.	09E	095	2C8	3A6	0F2	263	108	307	3E8	3C4	2BB	14C	36E	13E	2C9	376
28.	014	00F	0DA	133	163	05C	0AA	1E5	019	37D	043	1FC	184	07A	3FE	03D
29.	0FE	25F	26E	3B7	135	2E8	3B1	1B7	012	2CA	0C2	113	001	271	1D8	01A
2A.	16F	1C9	0AD	236	299	3CF	3EC	24E	3F0	1D4	3CC	2BF	2C3	338	1B5	25C
2B.	181	052	243	1F3	11F	2EE	332	32C	034	3A8	2B4	34F	031	305	006	124
2C.	13F	13C	19E	3A0	17C	2E2	3CE	345	3CD	0EF	205	31A	23D	06B	059	19F
2D.	1E0	3D8	3F9	103	337	0DB	14D	353	127	0CE	385	114	107	3D7	057	288
2E.	04F	2B2	2CB	039	234	2B5	2E1	32A	2FB	115	116	37B	3A5	092	373	17F
2F.	21E	2AB	37F	2FD	2ED	2BA	1EA	125	208	16E	33C	0A9	2F3	3C2	3C1	21D
30.	11A	0A4	3EA	047	157	25D	1D9	10A	16D	20E	098	2B1	340	22E	241	078
31.	1F5	0ED	31E	298	3A7	30C	1CF	05F	351	0E4	335	046	151	24C	1EE	235
32.	12E	2A6	1A5	061	3A1	29C	011	066	093	03A	38A	1F8	1F0	084	134	356
33.	225	20C	3D9	2E4	0A8	0BE	1FE	0FC	0C7	377	2F7	07C	074	045	1E8	05A
34.	36B	36F	37E	375	04D	1FA	257	13B	089	220	399	00B	158	2D5	068	280
35.	357	0DD	0BF	1B0	2A7	23B	255	3FC	00A	330	2A4	200	016	008	126	0A6
36.	09B	37A	284	2D4	0F3	28E	237	31D	0DF	368	386	060	374	31C	033	26A
37.	100	394	1F9	04B	391	39F	30B	00C	077	2EB	3E3	231	29B	049	202	224
38.	132	2DA	2A8	286	06A	189	130	13D	1EC	29D	104	387	32F	316	207	137
39.	0DC	02B	1D7	21A	354	39C	0B6	329	285	3A4	0D9	245	2B3	0D6	33E	252
3A.	0CB	1DB	172	296	192	04A	244	250	1F6	2AD	2C6	346	09D	388	328	3A3
3B.	2C7	3E7	29E	3C0	0D5	22A	1F4	168	3FD	242	102	3C5	0F8	251	264	2DF
3C.	27C	029	003	38B	10C	380	10D	295	303	197	1CD	219	13A	306	166	304
3D.	175	19A	0D8	28A	0A2	26F	3B8	1C2	148	30A	0B8	24D	1A7	121	15E	372
3E.	0B4	266	22F	2FE	0B0	055	01E	3AC	14A	2E0	34B	1D5	3E9	393	2E7	037
3F.	20F	0D7	1A8	1AB	16B	36A	352	204	2BD	08B	147	1AA	35F	03C	309	33D

Figure 5A. Specification of the modified S-box S_0.

http://dx.doi.org/10.5772/intechopen.70420

	..0	..1	..2	..3	..4	..5	..6	..7	..8	..9	..A	..B	..C	..D	..E	..F
00.	021	09B	37A	3AB	0DF	016	1FE	004	07C	3BE	141	397	300	185	00C	1A7
01.	2FA	3AA	235	0B9	003	3CF	14A	18F	356	363	055	2E4	168	0CF	373	379
02.	2CA	33B	16B	393	283	2E0	2B9	3E9	12F	247	3AD	07B	288	146	30F	3C8
03.	15C	01F	22C	0F8	10F	35D	367	343	1EC	047	008	062	2CF	019	36B	148
04.	0B4	2E3	25E	234	0D2	1F8	184	2FF	2EB	2BB	3A1	34F	312	10B	2EA	04D
05.	1B1	2FE	084	3CC	216	337	0D4	08D	21F	035	1F5	32A	1AA	182	24B	1BF
06.	245	257	01E	34E	375	197	292	1DD	14D	190	27E	18D	137	3A3	228	392
07.	010	34C	389	114	3B9	28B	325	210	1E7	30B	388	335	094	088	038	1C2
08.	305	38E	112	0AA	01B	260	3C1	104	30E	3D4	0EF	079	347	382	22E	09D
09.	1E6	087	278	20D	25B	060	215	2C6	3E0	0A1	3F9	179	252	1B5	105	368
0A.	029	1E9	2C4	2C5	037	233	204	133	3BD	20B	37D	1AE	115	116	1B2	2F3
0B.	266	333	08F	050	1B9	328	26F	1EA	1A9	0E6	291	2ED	05E	162	1EE	362
0C.	15B	351	20F	17D	08B	2D5	259	271	14F	2F5	011	3E7	14B	391	248	0B2
0D.	119	3CD	160	23E	06A	0D0	3C3	01C	171	3D3	349	061	16F	0FB	1DF	342
0E.	082	074	218	2E9	3B3	225	2F9	230	020	223	151	0C5	2A9	0FE	096	045
0F.	0F2	0DA	03A	015	049	370	14C	255	369	193	344	20E	164	3A6	03D	387
10.	24C	030	315	3CA	2EE	0C6	02C	203	107	0F1	3FE	244	26C	264	1C6	1C9
11.	0B1	090	36F	28F	1A3	19D	0BE	317	19B	25C	117	0ED	395	0BF	37E	3E4
12.	35C	3FB	103	2E6	36E	11E	213	279	316	38C	277	286	081	068	3D1	1F7
13.	3C5	095	2FC	09F	2B5	332	05C	38A	3B8	09E	2DD	358	19F	111	2A7	2B0
14.	091	329	106	10E	012	273	2EC	033	080	174	2DB	1C7	102	2D3	123	1B0
15.	03F	2D4	364	131	0A6	275	00A	386	052	3DC	339	11A	211	02A	27F	0DD
16.	318	27B	17B	2D7	1E4	285	144	269	3F4	1EF	093	3BB	307	08E	3B0	0EB
17.	209	2CB	0BB	3A5	129	0AC	027	028	3E6	0E5	221	125	159	2B7	0F9	37C
18.	054	32D	3F6	031	053	29F	23C	2A1	0D9	237	11D	232	1B3	1C1	380	2C1
19.	0C7	360	0D6	265	34A	17F	296	3E1	20C	0A2	1F6	207	0CB	040	1D5	026
1A.	200	121	134	2AB	2FB	272	0D7	07E	001	262	27A	1FF	299	3EB	1FA	0A8
1B.	253	006	128	195	14E	289	0F6	3A8	3D2	261	178	3E5	2C0	0B7	303	181
1C.	097	22A	32E	166	306	0FC	139	138	0F7	1AC	1FD	29B	0AF	041	2CC	0CA
1D.	23B	1F2	25D	0EC	314	20A	03C	338	3C6	0C0	158	28C	3E8	21E	06E	263
1E.	0C4	085	1BD	051	3E2	153	013	0F3	2B6	1A8	17C	2DC	2C7	3B7	33C	29E
1F.	0B5	27C	3F2	398	194	099	0A9	320	35A	366	2C2	05D	1F9	226	098	04E
20.	05A	3AC	33E	0E8	0A7	186	100	17E	126	32B	110	05F	1A5	390	3CE	1FC
21.	11F	3D6	3D5	13C	2BD	251	355	065	336	3DF	152	07A	086	1B6	308	188
22.	0DC	124	15F	075	2E7	39E	046	302	32C	2CE	1DA	3AF	267	066	394	12B
23.	06D	371	2AF	12A	378	319	24D	1D7	37F	3A2	21D	157	31A	3FF	238	2DA
24.	071	31B	256	3F3	33D	280	30C	08C	21C	058	1CD	2D6	165	3A0	077	354
25.	022	32F	359	2BC	374	1EB	30A	192	1CF	1BA	06B	0A0	177	183	28E	2A8
26.	29C	130	323	122	331	201	3B1	0BC	25A	0D8	34B	11B	24F	2E8	1F1	3F5
27.	31C	254	346	376	11C	000	243	0C8	381	0E9	22D	01A	161	3D0	07F	1E0
28.	295	175	04F	3C4	1AF	2A2	191	2F7	34D	36C	2E2	3D7	02E	3CB	0F5	2F6
29.	0C1	30D	025	1F3	01D	1D3	06C	13B	109	2DF	38B	31F	18C	0E1	231	10D
2A.	36D	3DB	377	1DB	16D	09C	024	242	072	39B	31D	2C9	149	206	089	0A3
2B.	0EA	057	250	2CD	38F	2A0	0B3	169	12D	309	2D8	2AD	3F0	3F1	1C8	043
2C.	268	2A3	1D6	28A	1CA	324	2AA	02F	1DE	3C7	0D3	274	147	219	02D	2B2
2D.	1D8	13F	383	3DA	3ED	26A	0AE	1DC	301	2A4	350	2F2	0AB	2A6	3D8	014
2E.	2D2	352	108	0E3	270	229	1A1	29D	1BE	06F	002	059	0A4	198	23A	044
2F.	064	258	348	39C	176	2B4	007	3C2	33F	217	287	073	3B2	15E	03B	167
30.	2B8	2D0	340	0F4	0BD	2F0	353	39A	18A	29A	399	246	1CB	02B	1A2	2E1
31.	3FC	212	1B7	032	281	357	120	048	322	3A9	3B6	33A	196	1BB	1FB	19A
32.	1E2	0AD	101	0F0	22F	227	0B6	345	0C2	220	07D	298	3EF	0B8	2F1	0DE
33.	304	0E4	202	0D1	21B	005	12C	0EE	13A	3BF	092	00D	05B	009	37B	365
34.	0DB	2AC	27D	39D	3A7	214	0CC	1AD	2E5	2DE	1D9	1E5	1C0	3DE	140	24A
35.	2B3	26B	1F0	3C0	3A4	04A	039	2C3	0BA	078	1D4	1E3	16A	145	170	2C8
36.	00B	35B	1AB	127	2BF	16E	2BE	241	1E1	063	334	2B1	136	3EE	384	1C5
37.	23D	2D1	042	372	3BA	1ED	0FA	327	0C9	018	1C3	396	3F8	26E	1BC	187
38.	034	3FD	310	118	1D1	076	22B	143	208	38D	39F	0D5	3B4	199	3C9	3B5
39.	0E2	13D	10A	284	156	150	173	155	3DD	15D	0CD	163	1A0	0C3	10C	341
3A.	180	1A6	321	00E	276	03E	25F	3EC	189	3E3	1D0	1CC	26D	205	17A	3FA
3B.	35E	036	35F	2F8	067	2BA	2A5	16C	3D9	2FD	297	18E	113	0FD	313	0E7
3C.	15A	1B8	08A	239	04B	326	083	385	2F4	19C	12E	017	3BC	224	135	290
3D.	09A	311	240	13E	0A5	24E	069	18B	0FF	236	36A	1A4	04C	3AE	1E8	31E
3E.	132	23F	222	070	2AE	3EA	249	023	293	0B0	330	21A	28D	1CE	154	172
3F.	1F4	056	00F	2EF	361	1D2	0E0	1C4	19E	282	1B4	3F7	294	142	2D9	0CE

Figure 6A. Specification of the secret S-box $\mathbf{S}_1$.

	..0	..1	..2	..3	..4	..5	..6	..7	..8	..9	..A	..B	..C	..D	..E	..F
00.	021	09B	37A	3AB	0DF	016	1FE	004	07C	3BE	141	397	300	185	00C	1A7
01.	2FA	3AA	235	0B9	003	3CF	14A	18F	356	363	173	2E4	168	0CF	373	379
02.	2CA	326	16B	393	283	2E0	2B9	3E9	12F	247	3D8	07B	288	146	30F	267
03.	15C	01F	22C	0F8	10F	35D	367	343	1EC	047	008	062	2CF	3D6	36B	148
04.	0B4	2E3	25E	234	0D2	1F8	184	2FF	2EB	2BB	3A1	34F	312	10B	2EA	04D
05.	1B1	2FE	084	229	216	337	0D4	08D	21F	035	164	32A	1AA	182	24B	1BF
06.	245	257	01E	34E	375	197	292	1DD	14D	190	27E	13D	137	3A3	228	392
07.	010	34C	389	114	3B9	28B	325	210	1E7	30B	388	1A1	094	088	038	1C2
08.	305	38E	112	0AA	01B	260	3C1	104	30E	3D4	0EF	079	347	382	22E	09D
09.	1E6	087	278	20D	25B	060	215	2C6	3E0	055	3F9	179	252	1B5	105	368
0A.	029	1E9	2C4	2C5	037	233	204	133	3BD	20B	37D	1AE	03D	116	1B2	2F3
0B.	266	333	08F	050	1B9	328	26F	1EA	1A9	0E6	291	2ED	05E	162	1EE	362
0C.	15B	351	20F	17D	08B	2D5	259	271	14F	2F5	011	3E7	14B	391	248	0B2
0D.	119	3CD	160	23E	06A	0D0	3C3	01C	171	3D3	349	061	16F	0FB	1DF	342
0E.	082	068	218	2E9	3B3	225	2F9	230	020	223	151	0C5	2A9	0FE	096	045
0F.	0F2	0DA	03A	015	049	370	14C	255	369	193	38A	20E	0B1	3A6	039	387
10.	24C	030	315	3CA	0A1	0C6	02C	203	107	115	3FE	244	26C	264	1C6	1C9
11.	123	090	36F	28F	1A3	19D	0BE	317	19B	25C	117	0ED	395	0BF	37E	3E4
12.	04C	3FB	103	2E6	3C8	11E	3D1	279	316	38C	277	286	081	074	213	1F7
13.	3C5	095	2FC	09F	2B5	332	05C	31F	324	09E	2DD	3FC	19F	111	2A7	2B0
14.	091	329	106	10E	012	273	2EC	341	080	174	2DB	1C7	102	2D3	2EE	1B0
15.	03F	2D4	364	131	0A6	275	00A	386	052	3DC	339	11A	211	02A	27F	0DD
16.	318	27B	17B	2D7	1E4	285	0AC	269	3F4	1EF	093	3BB	307	08E	3B0	0EB
17.	209	2CB	0BB	3A5	129	1CA	027	028	3E6	064	221	125	159	2B7	0F9	37C
18.	054	32D	3F6	031	053	29F	23C	2A1	0D9	237	336	232	1B3	1C1	380	2C1
19.	1DA	360	30C	265	34A	17F	296	3E1	20C	0A2	1F6	207	0F1	040	1D5	026
1A.	200	121	134	2AB	2FB	272	0D7	07E	001	262	27A	1FF	299	3EB	1FA	39F
1B.	253	006	128	36E	14E	289	0F6	3A8	3D2	261	178	3E5	2C0	0B7	303	181
1C.	097	22A	32E	166	306	0FC	139	138	3BF	1AC	1FD	29B	0AF	041	2CC	0CA
1D.	23B	1F2	25D	0EC	314	20A	03C	120	3C6	0C0	158	28C	3E8	21E	06E	263
1E.	0C4	085	1BD	051	3E2	153	013	0F3	2B6	1A8	17C	2DC	2C7	3B7	33C	29E
1F.	0B5	27C	3F2	398	194	099	0A9	320	35A	366	2C2	05D	1F9	226	098	04E
20.	05A	3AC	33E	0E8	0A7	186	1D8	17E	126	32B	110	05F	1A5	390	3CE	1FC
21.	11F	019	3D5	13C	2BD	251	355	065	1F5	3DF	152	07A	086	1B6	308	188
22.	0DC	124	15F	075	2E7	39E	046	302	32C	2CE	3CC	3AF	208	066	394	12B
23.	06D	371	2AF	12A	378	319	24D	1D7	37F	3A2	21D	157	31A	3FF	3B2	2DA
24.	071	31B	256	3F3	33D	280	144	08C	21C	058	1CD	2D6	165	3A0	077	354
25.	022	32F	359	2BC	374	1EB	30A	192	1CF	1BA	06B	0A0	177	183	28E	2A8
26.	29C	130	323	122	331	201	3B1	0BC	25A	0D8	34B	11B	24F	2E8	1F1	3F5
27.	31C	254	346	376	11C	000	243	0C8	381	0E9	22D	01A	161	3D0	07F	1E0
28.	295	175	04F	3C4	1AF	2A2	191	2F7	34D	36C	2E2	3D7	0F7	18B	0F5	2F6
29.	0C1	30D	025	1F3	01D	1D3	06C	13B	109	2DF	38B	2E5	18C	0E1	231	10D
2A.	36D	3DB	377	1DB	16D	09C	024	242	072	39B	31D	2C9	149	0F0	089	0A3
2B.	0EA	057	250	2CD	38F	2A0	0B3	169	12D	309	2D8	2AD	358	3F1	1C8	043
2C.	268	2A3	1D6	28A	3EC	18D	2AA	02F	1DE	3C7	0D3	274	147	219	02D	2B2
2D.	0CC	13F	383	3DA	3ED	26A	0AE	1DC	301	2A4	350	2F2	0AB	2A6	39A	014
2E.	2D2	352	108	0E3	270	3E3	02E	29D	1BE	06F	002	059	0A4	198	23A	044
2F.	0CB	258	348	39C	176	2B4	007	3C2	33F	217	287	073	238	15E	03B	167
30.	2B8	2D0	340	0F4	0BD	2F0	353	100	18A	29A	399	246	1CB	02B	1A2	2E1
31.	3F0	212	1B7	032	281	357	3AD	048	322	3A9	3B6	33A	196	1BB	1FB	19A
32.	1E2	0AD	101	033	22F	227	0B6	345	0C2	220	07D	298	3EF	0B8	2F1	0DE
33.	304	0E4	202	0D1	21B	005	12C	0EE	13A	0C7	092	00D	05B	009	37B	365
34.	0DB	2AC	27D	39D	3A7	214	338	1AD	335	2DE	1D9	1E5	1C0	3DE	140	24A
35.	2B3	26B	1F0	3C0	3A4	04A	0A8	2C3	0BA	078	1D4	1E3	16A	145	170	2C8
36.	00B	35B	1AB	127	2BF	16E	2BE	241	1E1	063	334	2B1	136	3EE	3B8	1C5
37.	23D	2D1	042	372	3BA	1ED	0FA	327	0C9	018	1C3	396	3F8	26E	1BC	187
38.	034	3FD	310	118	1D1	076	22B	143	38D	33B	0E5	0D5	3B4	199	3C9	3B5
39.	0E2	195	10A	284	156	150	11D	155	3DD	15D	0CD	163	1A0	0C3	10C	35C
3A.	180	1A6	321	00E	276	03E	25F	0D6	189	206	1D0	1CC	26D	205	17A	3FA
3B.	35E	036	35F	2F8	067	2BA	2A5	16C	3D9	2FD	297	18E	113	0FD	313	0E7
3C.	15A	1B8	08A	239	04B	384	083	385	2F4	19C	12E	017	3BC	224	135	290
3D.	09A	311	240	13E	0A5	24E	069	3CB	0FF	236	36A	1A4	344	3AE	1E8	31E
3E.	132	23F	222	070	2AE	3EA	249	023	293	0B0	330	21A	28D	1CE	154	172
3F.	1F4	056	00F	2EF	361	1D2	0E0	1C4	19E	282	1B4	3F7	294	142	2D9	0CE

Figure 7A. Specification of the modified S-box S_1.

http://dx.doi.org/10.5772/intechopen.70420

	..0	..1	..2	..3	..4	..5	..6	..7	..8	..9	..A	..B	..C	..D	..E	..F
00.	12E	38B	18E	131	039	10D	2DE	246	286	2BE	315	384	21D	1A5	06D	0CA
01.	2A2	2CE	264	085	374	3BB	3B9	1B7	0DE	3BC	207	002	392	1B5	0BA	318
02.	39C	2EE	13C	125	227	063	27E	126	0AA	082	305	15C	206	0A0	009	3C6
03.	100	3F3	2AD	199	102	108	1DB	30E	310	245	0A8	116	022	3C1	028	332
04.	1E1	2E7	0DA	255	0CB	07C	2A0	240	150	165	258	2C8	0C4	334	36B	2D1
05.	1E0	138	39A	0FF	1A7	10C	353	19B	171	038	3BD	000	3A2	1B8	282	2EB
06.	1D4	3D4	20F	23C	0D7	154	012	0DF	10F	237	04E	155	2E2	189	01E	121
07.	1B4	381	273	123	052	12C	158	033	2D2	3D3	23B	3B8	2F7	160	341	124
08.	337	1E6	3BE	327	0BD	096	2E4	107	1C2	263	2A4	2CF	244	196	36A	16D
09.	0A1	2C3	004	049	303	3A3	09E	361	065	1B0	05D	319	21B	249	2B2	399
0A.	198	26A	080	1B1	340	28A	33C	316	0FC	37F	1A8	134	17F	3DF	34F	3E5
0B.	2D9	32A	34A	1D1	09D	3FB	0BE	3A8	383	036	3B6	222	22E	2B6	3A6	0FA
0C.	1C1	0B2	113	3E8	129	34C	153	333	07E	01F	01D	213	299	0F8	130	1B9
0D.	182	0A2	1A1	1CD	119	210	24C	020	097	3F0	280	112	04C	14D	1EB	307
0E.	386	0AE	322	2FE	217	3D7	1AF	345	05B	3F5	110	1C8	03C	1C5	35A	0C0
0F.	3F1	238	338	1CB	0F4	2B4	00F	3A1	242	03D	1DA	1B3	003	114	3FA	313
10.	35F	0C5	261	2C1	15D	28F	390	1C9	1DD	3C7	14F	11D	066	04D	03B	0E9
11.	2BA	2FD	347	191	044	0B8	194	148	256	360	326	257	1AE	396	09B	2CD
12.	1E7	3CD	1FF	269	040	3E7	08A	216	0C9	33B	3D9	1BC	2B1	325	11B	16F
13.	053	22A	186	180	27D	11F	2A9	13E	3E1	0D4	24E	1D2	2FC	3C9	1FB	31A
14.	3DE	1D7	025	372	339	2C7	2ED	25F	3E6	098	2EF	247	0E8	2D3	105	09F
15.	2CC	36D	31F	24B	1D8	241	068	211	2AF	3EA	355	35C	026	2BD	0B5	0EF
16.	35B	233	05A	1BE	291	368	137	035	298	140	26B	1E4	379	07F	3EB	164
17.	20B	12D	375	1BF	12F	1AA	18B	268	3F4	364	0F7	057	0B9	3C5	060	19D
18.	22B	17C	11C	0B1	23A	3B4	05F	2F5	219	224	3CC	042	06F	39D	218	023
19.	215	177	190	395	274	359	0E2	2E9	397	0F1	010	099	17D	08E	314	317
1A.	0DC	03F	1AC	1A6	132	152	195	3AD	3E9	3C2	019	0F0	0CD	074	178	174
1B.	184	3E0	084	2FB	1A9	0B7	250	27B	06C	13B	0FB	296	297	30F	350	14E
1C.	007	10E	19C	055	351	034	175	103	272	02D	2C0	21C	047	20D	0E3	29B
1D.	13F	1DF	162	376	0BF	1CA	3EC	2B9	3FE	388	133	29D	33A	304	1FE	059
1E.	13D	19A	294	02B	127	1E8	275	07B	14C	018	031	15B	0A3	0EC	27C	087
1F.	38D	3B0	284	1FA	1F5	00A	3E2	02E	228	285	34B	311	075	2F1	1C4	094
20.	3FF	202	27F	2F9	30D	135	33F	301	3D8	2C6	3D2	309	0EA	073	1F1	289
21.	3B5	093	111	0B4	20E	1BA	1F7	24A	394	157	366	336	39B	017	25C	3C4
22.	1EC	2BC	144	1E9	193	16A	33D	344	295	079	2B7	2D4	38A	17A	292	0AC
23.	0F2	35E	1EF	0BB	1BB	071	2DA	3F7	3D1	037	2AB	330	0B0	2DB	07A	22D
24.	00C	149	0AF	290	2E0	122	283	32E	3AE	3C3	1D9	2E5	37B	0BC	265	32D
25.	089	2CB	115	081	18A	0E5	05C	1A3	287	0D0	276	32C	0C3	30B	226	1C0
26.	2F3	0A5	062	2AA	185	091	208	156	230	320	385	28E	21E	3F9	11E	05E
27.	159	281	0C8	37C	0DD	188	04F	26E	33E	2F8	3A0	3B3	3C8	0A9	1A2	3AA
28.	302	36E	38F	19E	212	142	24D	0B3	141	3EF	1CE	262	145	362	346	176
29.	1E3	14B	3A9	3DD	1C6	3F8	070	0D3	1EA	3BA	248	146	201	243	1F6	205
2A.	0A7	20A	2F6	00E	267	26D	2A7	31D	2D0	0D1	38E	006	30A	3E3	2C5	28B
2B.	2D5	3A7	1D5	3A4	101	2D7	34E	2B5	072	26C	090	1F8	1F9	3AF	1F0	0C2
2C.	2C2	21A	06A	0AB	1FC	109	16B	15E	161	38C	1CC	271	279	369	342	1D6
2D.	01A	016	352	173	34D	354	181	235	254	23F	16C	030	03E	1C3	2EA	0CF
2E.	18C	078	18D	01B	117	393	3F2	39E	37D	1BD	24F	10A	29A	0A4	08D	187
2F.	015	046	0C1	251	00D	348	014	21F	001	008	2CA	321	1B2	1B6	043	147
30.	223	0B6	054	1AB	0FD	373	31E	323	20C	151	10B	288	045	041	349	2E3
31.	32F	0ED	277	179	278	3F6	23E	252	077	04A	120	200	308	300	312	04B
32.	1ED	048	30C	183	0D2	39F	3B7	0AD	3FD	204	050	1C7	197	2F2	221	209
33.	1F3	343	051	1F2	169	266	25A	26F	0F3	2B0	095	17B	31B	0F6	0E6	2DC
34.	225	36C	1EE	253	058	0E1	021	31C	3D6	1AD	167	2AC	06B	23D	398	032
35.	35D	2FA	00B	391	239	0F5	335	02C	083	143	02A	29E	36F	214	104	14A
36.	0E4	1E5	19F	2E1	1FD	356	28D	07D	11A	0EE	0EB	370	358	1DC	163	056
37.	367	03A	2D6	363	229	3DA	08B	382	270	2E8	2FF	168	027	2AE	170	28C
38.	2A3	08C	1CF	076	389	32B	2EC	2A5	2C9	2A6	29C	3ED	09C	0CC	2A8	203
39.	0FE	293	29F	2F4	0E7	232	0CE	3AB	13A	011	3DB	220	0D8	1F4	22F	236
3A.	17E	1A4	27A	128	329	324	067	365	024	2B8	3E4	0D6	3AC	3A5	172	306
3B.	16E	0DB	3C0	25B	088	2D8	3BF	380	259	2A1	1E2	377	02F	029	2F0	2BF
3C.	2C4	136	2BB	3B1	1DE	3D5	01C	25E	2B3	069	0A6	106	0D5	3DC	118	2E6
3D.	2DD	1D3	18F	371	064	260	0C7	0E0	0C6	1D0	3EE	0D9	37A	387	3CB	234
3E.	3D0	15F	3B2	08F	15A	013	331	328	06E	25D	0F9	092	166	378	3CE	139
3F.	005	09A	12B	061	231	1A0	3CF	3CA	2DF	192	086	357	22C	12A	3FC	37E

Figure 8A. Specification of the secret S-box $\mathbf{S}_2$.

	..0	..1	..2	..3	..4	..5	..6	..7	..8	..9	..A	..B	..C	..D	..E	..F
00.	12E	38B	18E	131	039	10D	2DE	246	286	2BE	315	384	21D	142	06D	0CA
01.	2A2	2CE	264	085	374	3BB	3B9	1B7	3E6	3BC	207	002	392	1B5	0BA	318
02.	39C	2EE	1DA	125	019	063	27E	126	19A	082	305	0E3	206	0A0	009	3C6
03.	100	3F3	2AD	199	102	108	1DB	2F0	310	245	0A8	116	022	3C1	028	332
04.	1E1	2E7	0DA	2B7	0CB	07C	2A0	240	150	165	258	2C8	0C4	334	36B	2D1
05.	1E0	138	39A	0FF	1A7	10C	353	19B	171	038	3BD	000	3A2	1B8	282	2EB
06.	1D4	3D4	20F	23C	0D7	154	012	0DF	3A8	237	09E	155	2E2	189	2F2	136
07.	1B4	381	273	123	052	12C	158	033	2D2	3D3	23B	3B8	2F7	160	341	124
08.	337	1E6	3BE	327	1D3	045	2E4	107	1C2	263	2A4	2CF	244	196	36A	16D
09.	0A1	2C3	004	049	209	3A3	221	361	01E	1B0	05D	319	21B	249	2B2	399
0A.	198	26A	080	1B1	340	28A	33C	316	0FC	37F	1A8	134	17F	3DF	34F	3E5
0B.	2D9	32A	34A	1D1	09D	3FB	0BE	3EA	383	036	3B6	222	22E	2B6	3A6	0FA
0C.	1C1	0B2	113	3E8	129	34C	153	333	07E	01F	01D	213	299	0F8	130	1B9
0D.	182	0A2	1A1	3D5	119	10F	24C	020	097	3F0	280	112	04C	14D	1EB	307
0E.	386	0AE	322	2FE	0C5	3D7	1AF	345	05B	3F5	110	1C8	03C	1C5	35A	0C0
0F.	3F1	15B	338	1CB	0F4	2B4	00F	3A1	242	03D	29D	1B3	003	114	3FA	313
10.	35F	217	261	2C1	15D	28F	390	1C9	1DD	3C7	14F	11D	066	04D	03B	0E9
11.	2BA	2FD	347	191	044	0B8	194	148	256	360	326	257	1AE	396	09B	2CD
12.	1E7	3CD	1FF	269	040	3E7	08A	216	0C9	33B	3D9	1BC	2B1	325	11B	16F
13.	053	22A	186	180	27D	11F	2A9	13E	3E1	0D4	24E	1D2	2FC	3C9	1FB	31A
14.	3DE	1D7	025	372	339	2C7	2ED	25F	0A7	098	2EF	247	0E8	2D3	105	09F
15.	2CC	36D	31F	24B	1D8	241	068	211	2AF	0AA	355	35C	026	2BD	238	0EF
16.	35B	233	05A	1BE	291	368	137	035	298	140	26B	1E4	379	07F	3EB	164
17.	20B	12D	375	1BF	12F	1AA	18B	268	3F4	364	0F7	1CC	0B9	3C5	060	19D
18.	22B	17C	11C	0B1	23A	3B4	05F	2F5	219	224	0E5	042	06F	39D	218	023
19.	1DE	177	190	395	274	359	0E2	2E9	397	0F1	010	099	17D	08E	314	317
1A.	0DC	03F	1AC	1A6	132	152	195	3AD	3E9	3C2	1BB	0F0	0CD	074	178	174
1B.	184	3E0	389	2FB	1A9	0B7	250	27B	06C	13B	0FB	296	297	30F	350	14E
1C.	007	10E	19C	055	351	034	175	103	272	02D	2C0	21C	047	20D	0EA	29B
1D.	13F	1DF	162	376	0BF	1CA	3EC	2B9	3FE	388	133	0A9	33A	304	1FE	059
1E.	13D	0BD	294	02B	127	1E8	275	07B	14C	018	031	1C6	0A3	0EC	27C	087
1F.	38D	3B0	284	1FA	1F5	00A	3E2	02E	228	285	34B	311	075	2F1	1C4	094
20.	3FF	202	27F	2F9	30D	135	33F	301	3D8	2C6	3D2	309	057	073	1F1	289
21.	3B5	3CE	111	0B4	20E	1BA	1F7	24A	394	157	366	336	39B	017	25C	3C4
22.	1EC	2BC	144	1E9	193	16A	33D	344	295	079	027	2D4	38A	17A	292	0AC
23.	0F2	35E	1EF	0BB	106	071	2DA	3F7	084	037	2AB	330	0B0	2DB	07A	22D
24.	00C	149	0AF	290	2E0	122	283	32E	3AE	3C3	1D9	2E5	37B	0BC	265	32D
25.	089	2CB	115	081	18A	255	05C	1A3	287	0D0	276	32C	0C3	30B	226	1C0
26.	2F3	0A5	121	2AA	210	091	208	3EE	230	320	385	28E	21E	3F9	11E	05E
27.	159	281	0C8	37C	0DD	188	04F	26E	33E	2F8	3A0	3B3	3C8	227	1A2	3AA
28.	302	36E	38F	19E	212	13C	24D	0B3	141	3EF	1CE	262	145	362	346	176
29.	1E3	14B	3A9	3DD	093	3F8	070	0D3	1EA	3BA	248	146	201	243	1F6	205
2A.	1CD	20A	2F6	00E	267	26D	2A7	1FC	2D0	0D1	38E	006	30A	3E3	2C5	28B
2B.	2D5	3A7	1D5	3A4	101	2D7	34E	2B5	072	26C	090	1F8	1F9	3AF	1F0	0C2
2C.	2C2	21A	06A	0AB	1EE	109	16B	15E	161	38C	156	271	279	369	342	1D6
2D.	01A	016	352	173	34D	354	181	185	1A5	23F	16C	030	215	1C3	2EA	0CF
2E.	0DE	078	18D	01B	117	393	3F2	39E	37D	1BD	24F	18C	29A	0A4	08D	187
2F.	015	065	0C1	251	00D	348	014	21F	001	008	2CA	321	1B2	1B6	043	147
30.	223	0B6	054	1AB	0FD	373	31E	323	20C	151	10B	288	2DF	041	349	2E3
31.	32F	0ED	277	179	278	3F6	23E	252	077	04A	120	200	308	300	312	04B
32.	1ED	048	30C	183	0D2	39F	3B7	0AD	3FD	204	050	1C7	197	3BF	046	04E
33.	1F3	343	051	1F2	169	266	25A	26F	0F3	2B0	095	17B	31B	0F6	0E6	2DC
34.	225	36C	377	253	058	0E1	021	31C	3D6	1AD	167	2AC	06B	23D	398	032
35.	35D	2FA	00B	391	239	0F5	335	02C	083	143	02A	29E	36F	214	104	14A
36.	0E4	096	19F	2E1	1FD	30E	28D	07D	11A	0EE	0EB	370	358	1DC	163	056
37.	367	03A	2D6	363	229	3DA	08B	1E5	270	2E8	2FF	168	10A	2AE	170	28C
38.	2A3	08C	1CF	076	3D1	32B	2EC	2A5	2C9	2A6	29C	3ED	09C	0CC	2A8	203
39.	0FE	293	29F	2F4	0E7	232	0CE	3AB	13A	011	3DB	220	0D8	1F4	22F	236
3A.	062	1A4	27A	128	329	324	067	365	024	2B8	3E4	0D6	3AC	3A5	172	306
3B.	16E	0DB	3C0	25B	088	2D8	303	380	259	2A1	1E2	0B5	02F	029	356	2BF
3C.	2C4	03E	2BB	3B1	17E	3CC	01C	25E	2B3	069	0A6	15C	0D5	3DC	118	2E6
3D.	2DD	235	18F	371	064	260	0C7	0E0	0C6	1D0	254	0D9	37A	387	3CB	234
3E.	3D0	15F	3B2	08F	15A	013	331	328	06E	25D	0F9	092	166	378	31D	139
3F.	005	09A	12B	061	231	1A0	3CF	3CA	382	192	086	357	22C	12A	3FC	37E

Figure 9A. Specification of the modified S-box S_2.

http://dx.doi.org/10.5772/intechopen.70420

	..0	..1	..2	..3	..4	..5	..6	..7	..8	..9	..A	..B	..C	..D	..E	..F
00.	1AD	084	1B5	30A	25A	151	174	3F9	113	3B4	35B	291	332	170	021	31E
01.	00E	2FC	023	0B0	376	259	2BC	378	031	050	359	1FF	26C	0D5	214	0BD
02.	1AB	0AB	3AC	036	0E2	2F6	07A	0EA	2CB	0FE	24E	280	057	073	219	3EA
03.	2E2	27C	032	162	285	13C	0B6	1ED	0B3	2F5	2C6	34B	335	093	298	37A
04.	273	17E	30F	2E7	14B	3BC	1CE	039	315	01A	144	1C4	20A	3A9	362	10D
05.	235	1D9	2F9	0A4	052	0E3	17F	061	02C	140	0E1	156	10E	250	288	1BE
06.	07C	2B8	05D	242	192	0A8	3B0	0DB	129	2AF	063	3AF	3D1	0C8	0A6	029
07.	2B9	3B8	092	078	2A2	06E	2CF	3CF	0EF	0E7	019	1F1	07E	1BB	2C7	251
08.	36A	2CA	076	216	2E5	0E6	1DD	2FE	390	277	1D2	394	2C5	022	05A	396
09.	0F4	265	0FD	150	027	111	2EC	29C	3DF	11F	2A1	158	388	1D3	3C8	386
0A.	38B	279	064	1A4	028	34F	1D5	352	2C8	257	3C4	355	0B7	322	2C1	317
0B.	1DF	1A9	137	3DC	015	096	2AA	2A4	3F6	1A3	3DA	086	2E8	343	36F	11A
0C.	0A5	38D	328	348	292	308	3F4	059	31C	1AC	1E4	3BF	1C2	36D	1D8	0ED
0D.	191	3D3	3D4	046	0E8	373	034	23C	102	3C5	11E	393	00B	2D7	2DA	00F
0E.	209	230	19D	184	1B8	339	360	240	011	305	17A	324	344	045	3F0	0F3
0F.	1C6	0B4	08D	18E	035	0C9	345	0D3	37D	3CA	284	3EF	00D	197	36B	06B
10.	08B	10B	18A	218	3DE	32A	2CC	0AE	254	3FC	066	246	24D	232	0A2	145
11.	2DB	199	37F	1E1	392	3F3	1C8	1CD	136	2D0	325	27B	068	1F5	077	22D
12.	1E2	2F4	0B2	2E9	3CC	296	2EA	116	30D	276	02D	11B	09C	25E	157	195
13.	3A1	3F2	3D7	130	258	227	0D4	26B	1FB	1EA	379	329	179	2D5	0C4	09F
14.	39E	09E	1FD	15B	126	2B3	15E	012	21A	372	356	154	042	017	217	19B
15.	1F8	261	3ED	14A	22F	110	037	1B7	079	201	3C9	0EE	2B6	107	3CB	302
16.	19E	21D	1E5	205	25F	3BD	196	198	337	069	32E	0DF	3EE	272	0BC	3C2
17.	01D	37B	3C0	0A3	22E	123	2A9	0DE	2A7	2FF	3A5	05B	38F	047	1B4	350
18.	1EE	0A1	29D	1FC	024	29B	3A3	115	3BE	215	09A	37E	2A0	0C2	377	0B1
19.	149	04A	0E9	365	3D6	2E3	200	35A	17B	0D7	134	3D0	36E	336	334	1F6
1A.	1DC	3B2	2B1	2AB	3F1	1FA	067	06C	020	211	233	28D	0DA	34C	20C	1A8
1B.	28F	389	349	3F5	2FB	1CF	383	387	0CB	08F	0C0	135	3A7	2B0	346	30E
1C.	163	33C	32F	1EF	0FA	125	244	226	1C1	35E	1A2	252	1E9	3A0	146	3D8
1D.	148	353	0FF	37C	09D	2C0	268	048	117	1E3	2A6	003	323	0AD	1D7	313
1E.	072	18D	297	39A	0C7	12D	016	222	056	27A	287	095	366	293	3E0	354
1F.	369	299	190	10F	25B	183	080	1B6	361	3AA	3E1	318	2BA	15C	0D8	1DB
20.	342	2EE	1AE	04F	1A7	2CD	2F8	03A	01F	0BA	188	090	2B7	382	16F	0C5
21.	1B0	2D2	1CC	3B9	267	153	24B	1E7	0D2	0FC	33B	0F7	3BB	25C	1C7	0D9
22.	00C	271	0AA	1C5	357	1E8	01E	3FE	081	245	314	294	164	13F	212	340
23.	141	1B9	2C3	02E	087	0E4	13E	26A	171	249	22B	206	138	001	0A0	23F
24.	02B	2BB	06F	05E	275	20E	3B3	12A	28A	100	2AC	22A	263	0F9	1C0	21B
25.	203	303	35C	295	088	008	3E5	0DD	307	105	121	185	0A7	3EC	11C	347
26.	094	39D	1B2	02A	3B1	204	114	312	167	131	304	290	231	3E7	2D3	3D2
27.	2C2	32C	3E6	2F1	009	10C	327	2F2	2D1	1BA	2FD	35D	253	2EF	282	3D9
28.	338	14F	1B1	28B	330	2F0	18C	175	12E	169	2D9	223	2F3	255	0C3	13D
29.	398	15F	16D	2DC	2BD	0FB	3FA	2ED	147	161	01B	04B	17D	28C	058	3C1
2A.	1A6	21F	1DA	27F	124	2BF	39C	005	054	35F	143	3CE	19A	043	12F	104
2B.	0CF	286	18B	243	006	106	333	152	1BF	3FF	3B7	1EC	30B	098	08E	1D1
2C.	089	3CD	1F0	210	2EB	309	2F7	13B	20D	3AD	02F	0EC	11D	1BD	3A8	38E
2D.	311	1E6	3FB	0AF	2E1	12B	220	03D	0F1	2FA	208	16C	28E	181	33A	119
2E.	033	10A	0CA	2A5	010	31F	3BA	1F3	3B5	2DD	193	2AD	283	085	00A	32B
2F.	0F5	3AB	1D0	2E6	0EB	2DF	2B2	06A	065	38C	18F	364	33E	0B8	2CE	1F2
30.	289	142	266	132	3E2	24C	101	24A	39B	09B	097	1A0	229	375	320	062
31.	33D	118	3EB	03C	15A	281	1A1	207	3C7	331	319	082	127	34E	07B	239
32.	23A	300	0B5	01C	2B5	1E0	39F	180	321	133	26F	371	1B3	363	26D	23E
33.	0C6	165	0F6	19C	070	0E0	367	1DE	247	213	053	109	2D6	2B4	3DB	29E
34.	30C	1CB	0E5	1F7	15D	2E0	013	236	2A3	228	0BB	14D	018	278	155	1C9
35.	178	0CD	370	07D	3A6	23B	049	2D4	397	0BF	1BC	21E	399	3F8	0AC	004
36.	34A	055	04D	14C	33F	13A	301	05C	3A2	112	2DE	075	3F7	391	040	326
37.	2D8	000	0DC	0D1	041	14E	20B	1A5	166	168	051	22C	31B	0CC	16E	172
38.	1CA	2C4	3C3	0A9	03F	173	27E	08A	25D	1F9	014	17C	044	16B	380	176
39.	31D	3E9	108	139	2C9	04C	187	071	29F	381	316	038	0CE	06D	34D	1AA
3A.	122	2A8	1C3	04E	368	351	202	38A	225	189	194	306	026	0F0	248	08C
3B.	05F	19F	2BE	270	060	083	186	3DD	2AE	0C1	23D	160	241	0F8	1EB	385
3C.	374	177	3E4	358	1FE	099	120	1D4	3A4	310	030	1AF	1F4	0BE	074	16A
3D.	274	1D6	21C	3FD	3C6	238	234	262	3D5	31A	395	27D	3E8	128	002	29A
3E.	32D	0D0	341	26E	0B9	224	237	0F2	2E4	12C	103	025	20F	260	3AE	269
3F.	07F	03B	03E	007	182	159	091	3B6	3E3	384	264	0D6	36C	256	221	24F

Figure 10A. Specification of the secret S-box $\mathbf{S}_3$.

	..0	..1	..2	..3	..4	..5	..6	..7	..8	..9	..A	..B	..C	..D	..E	..F
00.	200	084	1B5	30A	25A	151	174	3F9	113	3B4	35B	291	332	170	021	31E
01.	00E	2FC	023	0B0	3A9	259	2BC	378	031	050	0D0	1FF	26C	0D5	214	23E
02.	1AB	0AB	3AC	036	0E2	2F6	07A	0EA	2CB	0FE	24E	280	138	073	219	3EA
03.	2E2	27C	032	162	285	13C	0B6	1ED	0B3	2F5	2C6	34B	335	1EF	26E	37A
04.	273	17E	30F	2E7	14B	3BC	1CE	039	315	01A	144	1C4	20A	17B	362	10D
05.	235	1D9	2F9	0A4	052	0E3	0BD	061	02C	140	0E1	156	10E	250	288	1BE
06.	07C	2B8	05D	242	192	0A8	3B0	0DB	129	2AF	063	3AF	3D1	0C8	0A6	029
07.	2B9	3B8	0D2	078	2A2	06E	2CF	3CF	0EF	0E7	019	1F1	07E	1BB	2C7	251
08.	36A	2CA	076	216	2E5	0E6	1DD	2FE	390	277	1D2	394	2C5	022	05A	396
09.	0F4	265	0FD	150	057	111	2EC	29C	3DF	11F	13A	158	388	1D3	3C8	386
0A.	38B	279	064	1A4	028	22F	1D5	352	2C8	257	3C4	355	104	322	2C1	382
0B.	1DF	1A9	137	3DC	015	096	2AA	2A4	3F6	1A3	3DA	086	2E8	343	233	11A
0C.	0A5	38D	328	348	292	132	3F4	059	31C	1AC	1C6	3BF	1C2	36D	1D8	0ED
0D.	191	3D3	3D4	3DE	0E8	373	034	23C	224	3C5	11E	393	00B	308	2DA	00F
0E.	209	230	19D	184	1B8	339	360	2D7	011	305	17A	324	344	128	3F0	0F3
0F.	317	0B4	08D	18E	035	0C9	345	0D3	37D	3CA	284	3EF	00D	197	36B	06B
10.	08B	10B	18A	218	046	32A	2CC	0AE	254	3FC	066	246	24D	232	0A2	145
11.	2DB	199	37F	1E1	392	3F3	1C8	1CD	136	2D0	325	27B	068	1F5	077	22D
12.	12F	2F4	0B2	2E9	3CC	296	2EA	116	30D	276	02D	266	09C	25E	157	195
13.	3A1	3F2	3D7	130	258	227	0D4	26B	027	1EA	379	329	179	2D5	0C4	09F
14.	39E	09E	1FD	15B	126	2B3	15E	012	21A	372	356	154	042	017	217	19B
15.	1F8	261	3ED	14A	1FB	110	037	1B7	079	045	3C9	0EE	2B6	107	3CB	302
16.	19E	21D	1E5	205	25F	3BD	196	198	337	069	32E	0DF	3EE	201	0BC	3C2
17.	01D	37B	3C0	0A3	22E	123	2A9	0DE	2A7	2FF	3A5	05B	38F	047	1B4	350
18.	0CB	0A1	29D	1FC	024	29B	3A3	2A1	3BE	215	09A	37E	2A0	0C2	377	0B1
19.	149	33B	323	365	3D6	2E3	082	35A	38C	0D7	134	3D0	36E	336	334	1F6
1A.	1DC	3B2	2B1	213	3F1	1FA	380	06C	020	211	033	28D	0DA	34C	20C	1A8
1B.	28F	369	349	3F5	2FB	1CF	383	387	35E	08F	29A	135	3A7	2B0	346	30E
1C.	163	33C	32F	093	0FA	125	244	226	1C1	1EE	1A2	252	1E9	3A0	146	3D8
1D.	148	353	0FF	37C	09D	2C0	268	048	117	1E3	2A6	003	11B	0AD	1D7	313
1E.	072	18D	297	39A	0C7	12D	016	222	056	1CB	287	095	366	293	3E0	354
1F.	13E	299	190	10F	25B	183	080	1B6	361	3AA	3E1	318	2BA	15C	0D8	1DB
20.	342	2EE	1AE	04F	1A7	2CD	2F8	03A	06A	0BA	188	090	2B7	1E4	16F	0C5
21.	1B0	2D2	1CC	3B9	267	153	24B	1E7	20B	0FC	2E6	0F7	3BB	376	1C7	0D9
22.	00C	271	0AA	1C5	357	1E8	01E	3FE	081	245	314	294	164	13F	212	340
23.	141	1B9	120	02E	34F	0E4	092	26A	171	249	22B	206	0C0	001	0A0	23F
24.	02B	2BB	06F	05E	275	20E	3B3	12A	28A	100	2AC	22A	263	0F9	1C0	21B
25.	203	303	35C	295	088	008	3E5	0DD	307	105	121	185	0A7	3EC	11C	347
26.	094	39D	1B2	02A	3B1	204	114	312	167	131	304	290	231	3E7	2D3	3D2
27.	2C2	32C	3E6	04A	009	10C	327	1BD	2D1	1BA	2FD	35D	253	2EF	282	3D9
28.	338	14F	1B1	28B	330	2F0	18C	175	12E	169	2D9	223	2F3	255	0C3	13D
29.	398	15F	16D	2DC	2BD	0FB	3FA	2ED	147	161	01B	04B	17D	28C	058	3C1
2A.	1A6	21F	1DA	0E9	124	2BF	39C	005	054	35F	143	3CE	19A	043	36F	1F3
2B.	0CF	286	18B	243	006	106	333	152	1BF	3FF	3B7	1EC	30B	098	08E	1D1
2C.	089	3CD	1F0	210	2EB	309	2F7	13B	20D	3AD	02F	0EC	11D	06D	3A8	38E
2D.	311	1E6	3FB	0AF	2E1	12B	220	03D	0F1	2FA	208	16C	28E	181	33A	119
2E.	109	10A	0CA	2A5	010	31F	3BA	0B7	3B5	2DD	193	2AD	283	085	00A	32B
2F.	2A8	3AB	1D0	2F1	0EB	2DF	298	1DE	065	17C	18F	364	33E	0B8	2CE	1F2
30.	289	142	2B2	0D6	3E2	24C	101	24A	39B	09B	097	1A0	229	375	320	062
31.	33D	118	3EB	03C	15A	281	1A1	207	3C7	331	319	27A	127	34E	07B	239
32.	23A	300	0B5	01C	2B5	1E0	39F	180	321	133	26F	371	1B3	363	26D	0F5
33.	0C6	165	0F6	19C	070	0E0	367	002	247	389	053	27F	2D6	2B4	3DB	29E
34.	30C	1AD	0E5	22C	15D	2E0	013	236	2A3	228	0BB	14D	018	278	155	1C9
35.	178	0CD	370	07D	3A6	23B	049	2D4	397	0BF	1BC	21E	399	3F8	0AC	004
36.	34A	055	04D	14C	33F	1F7	301	05C	3A2	112	2DE	075	3F7	391	040	326
37.	2D8	000	0DC	0D1	041	14E	067	160	166	168	051	0A9	31B	0CC	16E	172
38.	1CA	2C4	3C3	1E2	03F	173	27E	08A	25D	1F9	014	17F	044	16B	2F2	176
39.	31D	3E9	108	139	2C9	04C	187	071	29F	381	316	038	0CE	2C3	34D	1AA
3A.	122	225	1C3	04E	368	351	202	38A	102	189	194	306	026	0F0	248	08C
3B.	05F	19F	2BE	270	060	083	186	3DD	2AE	0C1	23D	272	241	0F8	1EB	01F
3C.	374	177	3E4	358	1FE	099	2AB	1D4	3A4	310	030	1AF	1F4	0BE	074	16A
3D.	274	1D6	21C	3FD	3C6	238	234	262	3D5	31A	395	27D	3E8	240	1A5	087
3E.	32D	359	341	25C	0B9	115	237	0F2	2E4	12C	103	025	20F	260	3AE	269
3F.	07F	03B	03E	007	182	159	091	3B6	3E3	384	264	385	36C	256	221	24F

Figure 11A. Specification of the modified S-box S_3.

http://dx.doi.org/10.5772/intechopen.70420

Author details

Arnaud Bannier and Eric Filiol*

*Address all correspondence to: filiol@esiea.fr

ESIEA—Operational Cryptology and Virology Lab (C+V)^{O}, France

References

[1] Filiol E. The Control of Technology by Nation States: Past, Present and Future—The Case of Cryptology and Information Security II. In: RusCrypto'2014, Moscow, March 25-28th, 2014

[2] Shumow D, Ferguson N. On the possibility of a back door in the nist sp800-90 dual ec prng. In: Proc. Crypto, vol. 7; 2007

[3] Strehle R. Verschlüsselt: der Fall Hans Bühler. Werd; 1994

[4] Fried J, Gaudry P, Heninger N, Thomé E. A kilobit hidden SNFs discrete logarithm computation. Cryptology ePrint Archive. Report 2016/961; 2016. http://eprint.iacr.org/2016/961

[5] Biham E, Shamir A. Differential Cryptanalysis of the Data Encryption Standard. Vol. 28. New York: Springer; 1993

[6] Schneier B. The nsa's cryptographic capabilities, 1998–2000. https://www.schneier.com/blog/archives/2013/09/the_nsas_crypto_1.html.

[7] Daemen J, Rijmen V. The Design of Rijndael. Heidelberg, Berlin: Springer Verlag; 2002

[8] Evertse J-H. Linear Structures in Blockciphers. Berlin, Heidelberg: Springer; 1988. pp. 249–266.

[9] Leander G, Abdelraheem MA, AlKhzaimi H, Zenner E. A cryptanalysis of printcipher: The invariant subspace attack. In: Advances in Cryptology—CRYPTO'. Berlin, Heidelberg, 2011. Berlin Heidelberg: Springer; 2011, pp. 249–266

[10] Knudsen L, Leander G, Poschmann A, Robshaw MJB. PRINTcipher: A Block Cipher for IC-Printing. Berlin Heidelberg: Springer; 2010, pp. 16–32

[11] Leander G, Minaud B, Rønjom S. A Generic Approach to Invariant Subspace Attacks: Cryptanalysis of Robin, iSCREAM and Zorro. Berlin, Heidelberg: Springer Berlin Heidelberg; 2015. pp. 254–283

[12] Grassi L, Rechberger C, Rønjom S. Subspace trail cryptanalysis and its applications to AES. IACR Transactions on Symmetric Cryptology. 2017;2016(2):192–225

[13] Todo Y, Leander G, Sasaki Y. Nonlinear Invariant Attack. Berlin, Heidelberg: Springer Berlin Heidelberg; 2016. pp. 3–33

[14] Rijmen V, Preneel B. A family of trapdoor ciphers. In: Fast Software Encryption. Springer; 1997. pp. 139–148

[15] Wu H, Bao F, Deng RH, Ye Q-Z. Cryptanalysis of rijmen-preneel trapdoor ciphers. In: Advances in Cryptology—Asiacrypt'98. Springer; 1998. pp. 126–132

[16] Angelova V, Borissov Y. Plaintext recovery in des-like cryptosystems based on s-boxes with embedded parity check. Serdica Journal of Computing. 2013;7(3):257–270

[17] Paterson KG. Imprimitive permutation groups and trapdoors in iterated block ciphers. In: Fast Software Encryption. Springer; 1999. pp. 201–214

[18] Caranti A, Dalla Volta F, Sala M, Villani F. Imprimitive permutations groups generated by the round functions of key-alternating block ciphers and truncated differential cryptanalysis. arXiv preprint math/0606022; 2006

[19] Harpes C. Cryptanalysis of iterated block ciphers [PhD thesis]. Diss. Techn. Wiss. ETH Zürich, Nr. 11625, 1996. Ref.: JL Massey; Korref.: U. Maurer; 1996

[20] Bannier A, Bodin N, Filiol E. Partition-based trapdoor ciphers. Cryptology ePrint Archive. Report 2016/493; 2016. http://eprint.iacr.org/2016/493

[21] Biham E, Shamir A. Differential cryptanalysis of DES-like cryptosystems. Journal of Cryptology. 1991;4(1):3–72.

[22] Matsui M. Linear cryptanalysis method for DES cipher. In: Advances in Cryptology—EUROCRYPT'93. Springer; 1994. pp. 386–397

[23] Knudsen LR, Robshaw MJB. The Block Cipher Companion. Heidelberg, Berlin: Springer; 2011

[24] Carlet C, Charpin P, Zinoviev V. Codes, bent functions and permutations suitable for des-like cryptosystems. Designs, Codes and Cryptography. 1998;15(2):125–156

[25] Nyberg K. Differentially uniform mappings for cryptography. In: Advances in Cryptology—Eurocrypt'93. Springer; 1993. pp. 55–64

[26] Krasner M, Kaloujnine L. Produit complet des groupes de permutations et problème d'extension de groupes. iii. Acta Sci. Math. (Szeged). 1951;14:69–82

[27] Leander G, Poschmann A. On the classification of 4 bit s-boxes. In: Arithmetic of Finite Fields. Heidelberg, Berlin: Springer; 2007. pp. 159–176

[28] Bannier A, Filiol E. Mathematical backdoors in symmetric encryption systems: Proposal for a backdoored AES-like block cipher. In: 1st International Workshop on Formal methods for Security Engineering (ForSE); February 2017

[29] Bannier A, Filiol E. Operational cryptanalysis based on backdoors exploitation in an AES-like cipher. In: RusCrypto'17; March 2017

[30] Daemen J, Rijmen V. Probability distributions of correlation and differentials in block ciphers. Journal of Mathematical Cryptology. 2007;1(3):221–242

[31] Bannier A, Filiol E. One construction of a backdoored aes-like block cipher and how to break it: proposal for a backdoored AES-like block cipher. RusKrypto Conference 2017; 2017. http://www.ruscrypto.ru/resource/summary/rc2017/02_filiol.pdf

[32] Bannier A, Filiol E. Mathematical backdoors in symmetric encryption systems: Proposal for a backdoored AES-like block cipher. International Workshop on FORmal Methods in Security Engineering (ForSE) 2017; 2017